CU00657873

Jesus, the Man and the Myth

Jesus, the Man and the Myth:

A Jewish Reading of the New Testament

Second edition, revised

Frederic Seager

Jesus, the Man and the Myth

Copyright 2021 © by Frederic Seager

All rights reserved. No part of this book may be used or reproduced by any means, graphic, electronic or mechanical, including photocopying, recording, taping or by any information storage retrieval system without the written permission of the author except in the case of brief quotations in critical articles or reviews.

ISBN:9798736148233

Table of Contents

Preface

My first encounter with Jesus goes back many years, to my early childhood. We were a few Jewish kids, seven or eight years old, playing in the park. Along came a group of Catholics from a local parochial school, who taunted us with repeated cries of "Christ killers! Christ killers!" The young priest accompanying the class smiled broadly. His pupils had learned their lesson well.

Even at that tender age, I reasoned that a religion that teaches hatred cannot be any good. I still hold to that belief. Some years later, in graduate school, I put the question to a fellow Ph.D. candidate in history, a Mennonite: how can Christians go on teaching that the Jews were responsible for the crucifixion? He answered simply: "But you *did* kill him." End of story – for one pious Christian, at least.

Among Gentiles who do not openly accuse the Jews of deicide, there seems to be a consensus that Jesus introduced a doctrine superior to Judaism. A Protestant lady attending an interfaith gathering in Geneva was surprised to learn that he had not invented the commandment to love one's neighbour as oneself. I explained that it first appeared in the book of Leviticus, chapter 19, verse 18. Just think of the First World War, I suggested; it ended in 1918. That way, you can't miss. Taken aback, she insisted that Jesus surpassed Jewish morality, since he told his disciples to love their enemies. Do you love your enemies? I asked. No, she admitted, but she was trying. For all I know, she may be trying still.

Atheists seem to share with liberal Protestants the view that Jesus was essentially a great moral innovator. An atheistic colleague (baptized Protestant) once tried to convince me what a wonderful person "J. C." was. My colleague was in good company: R. Travers Herford, the Unitarian minister who did more than any other Christian to rehabilitate the Pharisees, called Jesus "simply the greatest man who ever lived."[1] Richard Dawkins, who proudly denies the existence of God, claims that "Jesus is a huge improvement over the cruel ogre of the Old Testament." He proposes to create an association called "atheists for Jesus."[2]

The Jesus story naturally puts the Jews and Judaism in a bad light. Some web sites (fortunately few in number) portray the Jewish people as his sworn enemies, even today. This accusation is usually based on three verses in the New Testament: John 7, 1 and 11, 53-54, plus I Thessalonians 2, 14-16. Yet open anti-Semitism may not be the main problem here. In contemporary culture, Jews are often presented as poor benighted souls who rejected "the greatest man who ever lived" and worship a "cruel ogre" instead. No wonder the goyim (Gentiles, non-Jews) tend to look down on us.

To counter any negative impression, Jewish apologists (and some Christian) now present Jesus as a pious, if sadly misunderstood, Jew. They seem to believe that their efforts will lead to a decline in anti-Semitism. Yet the fact remains that the Jews who actually knew Jesus overwhelmingly rejected his message and that their descendents continue to do so. The message was a simple one: the kingdom of heaven is at hand; and if you accept me as your king, I will ensure that it comes to pass. The prospect of a divine kingdom about to be established on earth certainly had great initial appeal to most Jews in Roman-occupied Judea. When Jesus arrived in Jerusalem one fine Sunday in the spring, he received a rapturous welcome. The crowds lining his route prepared the way for him by laying palm branches on the ground and cried, "Hosanna to the Son of David!"[3] Five days later, he was dead. His popular following had largely disappeared.

So we are entitled to ask why Jesus was rejected by his compatriots, and why Jews ever since (except for the splinter group that helped to found Christianity) have tended to ignore his doctrine. This is a historical question. History is the science of causality, and it is for the historian to explain what caused the rift between Jesus and his fellow Jews. The great Salo W. Baron, author of a magisterial series of volumes on Jewish history, remarks laconically, "The bulk of the Jews . . . had to oppose Jesus."[4] But he does not say why, and other Jewish historians prefer to avoid the subject altogether,[5] leaving it to Bible scholars, theologians and other zealous amateurs.

Contemporary Jews, who are generally unfamiliar with the politics of Jesus's day, are more sensitive to moral issues when dealing with him. Shortly after the Second

World War, a French rabbi, in an effort to dissuade Jews from converting to Christianity, undertook to demonstrate that the ethics and morality of the Gospels are in no way superior to those of Judaism – rather the reverse.[6] While not entirely free of errors, his book represents a valiant attempt to set the record straight. It has been out of print for more than half a century and does not seem to attract many Jews, even those who read French. France is a predominantly Catholic country, and its Jewish minority no longer feels the need to refute missionary arguments. Since the second Vatican council, the Church of Rome has shown itself to be far more interested in recovering lapsed Catholics than in converting Jews.

The United States, on the other hand, is home to at least 900 evangelical Protestant congregations dedicated to saving the souls of Jews by having them acknowledge Jesus as their true saviour. The evangelicals are convinced that unless all Jews convert, Jesus will not return to fulfill his mission. Their intense missionary activity has led to a defensive reaction among Jews, several of whom have written books explaining how to refute the time-worn claims that Jesus was the Messiah foretold by Hebrew prophesy.[7] Detailed Biblical exegesis is the main feature of these refutations, which show that Christianity interprets the Hebrew Scriptures in a way totally inconsistent with Jewish tradition. This is true enough, but more is needed: first, a coherent analysis of the Nazarene's ministry and his compatriots' reaction to it; second, an explanation of his moral teachings and their relevance, if any, for the problems of our own day.

To understand both questions, one has to read the New Testament, and especially the Gospels. Despite their many inconsistencies, these narratives provide a key to understanding why Jesus's mission among his fellow Jews, despite some initial successes, eventually failed.[8] The evangelists faced a daunting task. First, they had to convince their readers that Jesus was indeed the Messiah foretold by the Hebrew prophets. Then, they had to show how popular he was among the people. Here, the "people" are none other than the Jews of Judea, except that the Nazarene's supporters are never referred to in the Gospels as Jews. The "people" become Jews only after he begins to lose popular support; then, nearly all Jews are portrayed his enemies, especially in the gospel according to John. Nonetheless, the Gospels remain a valid historical source – provided that we situate the Jesus story in its true context, that of a Jew and his relation to other Jews at a particular time and place in history.

What follows, then, is a Jewish reading of the Christian Scriptures. Christians read them differently, as they must, in order to seek spiritual inspiration and guidance in their holy book. The more enlightened among them tend to skip the hateful passages and concentrate instead on those of moral worth, not realizing that the latter are all derived from Judaism. Jews are usually discouraged from reading this remarkable work of anti-Jewish propaganda. Rabbis of all persuasions have long assumed that their congregants lack sufficient discernment to approach it critically. The present author ran into such opposition in his youth as a graduate student in history, when he casually remarked to his local rabbi that Jews could benefit from reading the New Testament. The rabbi, a luminary of Reform Judaism and noted Talmudic scholar, smiled condescendingly and replied, "We don't want to lose you."

The rabbi was apparently unaware that the young Ph.D. candidate had already read the New Testament, without being lost to Judaism as a result. He had encountered a Protestant missionary, who gave him a copy of the "Old Testament prophesy edition," a version replete with references to the Jewish Bible. These are not only prophetic, but include all possible similarities between the two sets of Scripture. Thus, the well-known phrase attributed to Jesus, "You have heard that it was said, 'You shall love your neighbour and hate your enemy.' But I say to you . . ."[9] bears the footnote, Lev. 19, 18. Yet when we turn to the book of Leviticus, we read simply: "You shall not take vengeance or bear a grudge against any of your people, but you shall love your neighbour as yourself. I am the Lord." There is absolutely nothing here about hating one's enemy. To the contrary, Jews are exhorted to show kindness and forbearance to those who hate them. "When you encounter your enemy's ox or ass wandering, you must take it back to him. When you see the ass of your enemy collapsing under its burden and would prefer not to raise it, you must nonetheless help him to raise it."[10] And again: "If your enemy is hungry, give him bread to eat. If he is thirsty, give him water to drink."[11] The Jewish reader of Matthew can only conclude that when Jesus claimed that

Judaism teaches hatred, he either was dishonest or simply did not understand the Bible.

The "Old Testament prophesy edition" is available in several languages, including Hebrew. For many years now, the State of Israel has been the target of Christian missionaries who believe that Jesus cannot return to earth until all Jews are reassembled in the Holy Land and accept him as their saviour. They distribute the Hebrew version of the "Old Testament prophesy edition" to impressionable young Israelis in the hope of making converts. An eleven-year-old pupil at a school belonging to the National Religious Party was severely reprimanded by his teacher for having kept his copy. The teacher snatched the book from his hands and burned it in front of the entire class.[12] Such a bigoted approach is all too common in Orthodox Judaism.

Preventing Jews from reading the Christian Scriptures is typical of a certain ghetto mentality which seeks to insulate Jews from Christianity. But the Jesus myth reaches them subliminally through the mass media and films, which portray him as a great hero. British journalist Jonathan Freedland was raised in an observant, kosher home. His Jewish education included regular synagogue attendance and Hebrew classes twice a week. Yet Jesus entered the household through television programs shown during Easter week. "I was watching Robert Powell get crucified when I should have been preparing the Seder table," he recalls. To this day, he admits being "strangely drawn to the story of Jesus. . . . [it] makes for gripping entertainment." The Jesus of film and television is portrayed as "a radical firebrand, whom the powerful want to silence and shut down."[13] What could be more appealing to an idealistic young Jew?

In recent times, Reform Judaism in the United States has shown a certain willingness to take on the New Testament. It is the subject of a course given at the Hebrew Union College by Rabbi Michael J. Cook, who has published a book encouraging Jews to "engage," as he puts it, the Christian Scriptures. He has a positive view of Jesus, calling him "a great teacher of Jewish ethics," but adds: "He was not the Messiah because he did not bring about independence for the land of Israel from Roman oppression."[14] A devout Christian would no doubt reply that, yes, Jesus did not liberate Judea, but that is because his own people rejected him as their king. Instead, by giving up his own life, he accomplished something far more remarkable: he redeemed all of humanity from original sin. Of course, if you want to be redeemed, you must first believe in him. Besides, the Christian may well ask: if Jesus was a great teacher of Jewish ethics, why not accept him now?

Most Jews would be at a loss to answer that question. For over a century and a half, liberal Judaism has reclaimed Jesus for the Jewish people and Jewish history. Rabbi Abraham Geiger, a leading founder of the Reform movement in Germany, wrote in 1864 that Jesus was not only a Jew, but a Pharisee as well.[15] This last assertion infuriated Protestant theologians of his time, but has been reaffirmed by other Jewish scholars. Baron notes simply that "Jesus appears as an essentially Pharisaic Jew."[16]

Some Orthodox Jewish leaders, in the interest of improved relations with Christians, now recognize Jesus as one of their own. American rabbi Irving Greenberg, a Jew of strict observance and an ardent Zionist, is at great pains to emphasize that Jesus was not a false Messiah, but simply a "failed Messiah," i.e. one "who has the right values and upholds the covenant but does not attain the final goal."[17] But did he have the right values, and did he uphold the covenant? That is the question under examination here.

Jesus was certainly a Jew, indeed a Jewish nationalist. This has endeared him to many Zionists, beginning with Joseph Klausner, a Jew living in Palestine under the British mandate, whose biography of Jesus appeared (in Hebrew) in the early 1920s. Klausner is quick to note the Nazarene spoke only Aramaic and that Galilee, where he exercised the better part of his ministry, "was the stronghold of the most enthusiastic Jewish patriotism."[18] If Jesus were alive today, he would obviously be an Israeli and most likely a militant of the religious Right. This is hardly a reason to venerate him. For a time, Israeli prime minister Ariel Sharon was also hailed by his followers as the King of Israel; but that does not, in itself, qualify him as the Messiah.

So why should Jews in our time try to understand Jesus? As long as Jewish communities lived their separate lives apart from mainstream Christian society, they could safely ignore him. Relations with Gentiles were limited to the business and administrative spheres. Now that Jews participate fully in that society and enjoy friendly relations with Christians, however, allusions to Jesus and the mythology surrounding him often crop up in everyday conversation. First, there are the trite expressions such as "Touch wood" or "Cross your fingers," along with superstitions like Friday the thirteenth. More seriously, it is not uncommon to hear the Biblical verse "An eye for an eye and a tooth for a tooth,"[19] quoted as if it sanctioned vengeance or reprisal. This is how Jesus interpreted it.[20] Yet how many Jews know the true meaning of the original text?

Casual conversations between ordinary Jews and Christians differ greatly from those formal interfaith meetings involving rabbis and members of the Christian clergy. In the latter, everyone is on his best behaviour and scrupulously avoids stepping on other people's toes. Among the laity, the tone is apt to be more direct. "But Jesus is love. You're not against love, are you?" Or this: "Wouldn't it be nice if we acted like one big family? After all, most religions are pretty much the same." Jews tend to brush off such well-meaning remarks without comment; they don't want to be called party-poopers. Besides, there is usually no rabbi or Jewish academic around to coach them.

The acid test of Judeo-Christian relations is in marriage. Rabbis, especially the Orthodox, see mixed unions as a trap for the Jewish partner. Jonathan Sacks, former Chief Rabbi of the United Kingdom, waxes eloquent over what he calls the Judeo-Christian tradition and Judeo-Christian values.[21] He is especially fond of the "Christmas spirit."[22] At the same time, he is convinced that "out-marriage" will necessarily lead to the demise of

Judaism.[23] We do not share this pessimistic approach. Mixed marriages do not have to result in the absorption of Jews into the great mass of Christendom. Rather, they can serve to lead Christians – not only spouses, but their families and friends – to a better understanding of Judaism. But first, Jews will need a thorough grounding in Judaism themselves, so that they can disentangle fact from fiction in the New Testament. Such is the aim of this essay.

I: A Serious Misunderstanding

"What do you think of Jesus Christ?" innocently asks the Christian maiden of her Jewish suitor. He flounders. "I wasn't there. . . . Maybe we've been waiting 5,700 whatever years, and this guy has been here and gone. I mean, I don't know." In other words, Jesus was not the Messiah foretold by the Hebrew prophets, and the world is hardly a better place for his brief passage. This is the usual argument that Jews fall back on when questioned about Jesus. It recalls the medieval disputations between rabbis and Christian clerics, each trying to prove the validity of his religion. Rabbis would point out that the Messiah was supposed to usher in an endless period of peace and universal happiness, in which, among other blessings, women would no longer experience pain in childbirth. Inasmuch as war is still prevalent and women still must endure pain when giving birth, the messianic age clearly has not yet arrived.

Few, if any, Christians would disagree with the rabbis' conclusion. Christianity postulates that the messianic age will not arrive until Jesus returns to earth; and for that to happen, all Jews will have to accept him as their saviour. Evangelicals want the second coming to take place as soon as possible; other Christians prefer to wait, secure in the belief that the Nazarene created a new morality based on love. This is the point of the young lady's question. She is obviously attracted to her Jewish suitor and would like to marry him. But she wants to know where he stands on the all-important question of love. All her beau manages to answer is that he cannot accept Jesus because of the humiliation Jews have had to suffer throughout the centuries in his name.[24]

On this last point, his attitude may be commendable; but it is hardly relevant in our time, for the simple reason that Jews are no longer being humiliated. The release in 2004 of Mel Gibson's openly anti-Semitic film, *The Passion of the Christ*, did not provoke a wave of persecution – either in the United States, where it was produced, or elsewhere. Nearly all Jews denounced the movie, as is only natural. They do not enjoy being called Christ-killers. Yet no one prevented them from going about their daily lives in peace. Nor were they the victims of aggression during the Easter season, as was too often the case until quite recently in Central and Eastern Europe.

Much of the credit for this welcome change belongs to the French historian, Jules Isaac. His ground-breaking book, *Jésus et Israël*, which appeared shortly after the Second World War, relies on the Gospels to show that the Nazarene often enjoyed widespread support among his compatriots in Judea. The author saw Jesus as a resistance fighter against Roman oppression and considered the priestly caste, as collaborators with Rome, largely responsible for his death.[25] In his efforts to clear Jews in general of the crime of deicide, Isaac won the support of liberal Protestant leaders in Europe and obtained a sympathetic audience with Pope John XXIII. Finally, in October 1965, Pope Paul VI issued a declaration which, while blaming the religious authorities in Judea for the crucifixion (a Roman punishment, by the way), absolves Jews in general, and especially those in our day. This clarification has not trickled down to all Catholics – certainly not to Gibson – but the image of Jews as Christ-killers does seem to be fading.

Indeed anti-Semitism has been in general decline for at least half a century. The horrors of the Nazi genocide may have given pause to those who used to blame the Jews for all the ills of this world. At the very least, the remarkable efficiency of the slaughter would seem to indicate that the victims were perhaps not quite so powerful as was formerly believed. The collapse of the Soviet empire finally laid to rest the myth of an international Judeo-Bolshevik conspiracy. Perhaps most importantly, Christianity itself is steadily losing believers. As evangelical congregations attract millions of poor souls looking for a quick fix to their personal problems, the more intelligent and better educated Christians continue to slip away from the established churches. It is the latter who tend to mingle socially with Jews and, in some cases, to marry them. These people are not interested primarily, if at all, in salvation after death. They seek to give meaning to their earthly lives and to life in general. Being disappointed with traditional religion, they look to Jesus as a role model.

There seems to be a Jesus for each and every one. For most Christians (including the Pope, who appeals for peace every year at Christmas), Jesus was a great pacifist, the "prince of peace," Yet he obviously did not see himself in this light. "Do not think that I have come to bring peace to the earth; I have not come to bring peace, but a sword. For I have come to set a man against his father, and a daughter against her mother, and a daughter-in-law against her mother-in-law; and one's foes will be member's of one's own household."[26]   This is the man on whom so many rely to uphold family values. They might meditate on Jesus's curt refusal to allow one of his disciples to attend his father's funeral. "Follow me, and let the dead bury their own dead."[27] Then there is the ecological Jesus. Some environmentalists would ask rhetorically: "What kind of car would Jesus drive?" They might inquire as to whether the man who killed a fig tree because it did not bear fruit out of season[28] was really a friend of nature.

Many Palestinians see Jesus as one of their own. During a press conference held at the Palais des Nations in Geneva on 2 September 1983, Yasser Arafat referred to Peter as a Palestinian fisherman who went to Rome (without being able to speak either Latin or Greek) and won its people over to his cause. He added that Jesus was the first Palestinian *fedayeen* (freedom fighter).[29] Arafat's followers like to embellish on this theme, calling Jesus the first Palestinian martyr, persecuted – as is to be expected – by the Jews.[30] Actually, the closest comparison to present-day Palestinians in the ancient world would be the Canaanites, the original inhabitants of Judea, for whom Jesus expressed open contempt.[31]

Feminists too often find Jesus to their liking. Maureen Dowd, columnist for the *New York Times*, writes: "In the New Testament, Jesus is surrounded by strong women. . . ."[32] She fails to mention who these strong women might be, and one looks in vain for any reference to them in the Christian Scriptures. The twelve apostles were all men. Nearly all the women mentioned in the Gospels, including the Nazarene's mother, are acted upon; they do not act. One woman especially close to Jesus was Mary Magdalene, from whom he exorcised no fewer than seven demons,[33] meaning that she was quite mad. Usually, folly is not equated with strength; but Ms. Dowd has some accounts to settle with the Vatican for not allowing women to play a more important role in church affairs. So she calls upon Jesus, as do many other Christians who, for one reason or another, are dissatisfied with the policies of their ecclesiastical hierarchies. Jesus is invoked as the standard from which established churches are presumed to have deviated.

Strong women can be found in the Jewish Bible, the most remarkable being Deborah, the prophetess who ruled over the Israelites for a time. As their commander-in-chief, she organized a great military victory over the Canaanite army.[34] Ruth, the Moabite, showed exemplary courage and loyalty by remaining with her Israelite mother-in-law after her husband's death, saying: "Wherever you go, I will go; wherever you dwell, I will dwell; your people shall be my people, and your God my God."[35] No less courageous was Esther, who hid her Jewish identity in order to marry the King of Persia and then used her position to denounce his prime minister, Haman, who was planning to kill all the Jews in the kingdom.[36]

If the great heroines of Judaism seem to merit little attention among feminists, it is probably because the Bible in which they appear is commonly called the "Old Testament." Being old, it must be out of date – or so it is widely assumed. After all, this year's model is deemed to be better than last year's, and next year's model will surely surpass this year's. If this were not so, we would keep our cars and household appliances until they wore out; and that would hardly do the economy any good. Manufacturers of toothpaste, disposable diapers, laundry detergent etc. regularly add the word "new" to their packaging. The tactic is often successful: it can result in increased sales. So if new is necessarily better, the "New" Testament has to be an improvement on the Old. Except that it isn't

Elisabeth Badinter, wife of a former French minister of justice, has written a book about love in which she adopts this Hegelian approach. She claims that there was no love in ancient times, and certainly not in the "Old Testament," but Jesus changed all that. All by himself, he introduced love to the world. That a Jewish woman, widely regarded as an intellectual, should spout such nonsense illustrates the sorry state of Jewish education in our time. Apparently Madame Badinter never learned that Judaism teaches love. She seems to think that the commandment to love one's neighbour originated with the Nazarene (whom she refers to as Christ). "Guided by the revolutionary [sic] principle of love," she writes, Jesus liberated women from slavery to their husbands.[37] Actually, by opposing divorce,[38] he did just the opposite. Most divorce actions are initiated by women, who would be truly enslaved if they had to remain imprisoned in a loveless marriage. In the Pentateuch, the husband divorces his wife, not the reverse.[39] The Pharisees (with whom we shall deal later) corrected this imbalance by allowing the wife to sue for divorce.

The belief that Jesus somehow invented love is no less erroneous for being general. Nineteenth-century English philosopher John Stuart Mill was astonished to find the commandment to love one's neighbour as oneself in the Pentateuch.[40] He apparently had believed that it was first uttered by Jesus, as do most Christians, even today. His atheistic compatriot Richard Dawkins belittles the commandment, since it applies only to fellow Israelites. He willfully ignores another commandment, a few verses further on, to love the stranger as oneself. "When a stranger resides with you in your land, you shall not wrong him. The stranger who resides with you shall be to you as one of your citizens; you shall love him as yourself, for you were strangers in the land of Egypt: I am the Lord."[41]

Loving, or at least befriending, the stranger is at the very heart of Jewish morality. This cannot be the fruit of spontaneous generation, a set of lofty principles impossible to fulfill, but is instead derived from human experience. The Israelites are commanded to love the stranger precisely because they were not so loved. Their tribulations as slaves in Egypt should prevent them from inflicting similar hardships on others. Elsewhere in the Pentateuch, the commandment is not limited to resident aliens, but applies to all foreigners, "for you know the feelings of the stranger, having been yourselves strangers in the land of Egypt."[42]

Jesus would have none of this. Jewish nationalist that he was, his attitude toward Gentiles ranged from calculated indifference to undisguised contempt. His instructions to the apostles leave no room for doubt: "Go nowhere among the Gentiles, and enter no town of the Samaritans, but go rather to the lost sheep of the house of Israel. As you go, proclaim the good news: the kingdom of heaven is at hand."[43] For the Jews, that is. The *goyim* will simply have to fend for themselves. He further advised his followers not to pray like Gentiles, who "repeat empty phrases" in the hope that "they will be heard because of their many words."[44] Even those pagans who were ready to adopt Judaism did not interest the Nazarene. He ridiculed the Pharisees, claiming that they "cover land and sea to make a single proselyte."[45]

"Do not give what is holy to dogs; and do not throw your pearls before swine," was the rule he laid down.[46] In plain terms, this means: do not attempt to enlighten the Gentiles or do them any favours. Having established his reputation as a faith healer, Jesus was approached by a Canaanite woman, a Gentile, who beseeched him to cure her daughter. He refused; for him, Jews had priority. "Let the children be fed first, for it is not fair to take the childrens' food and throw it to the dogs." He left no doubt that the *goyim* are no better than dogs. But the Canaanite woman was not intimidated. "Sir," she replied, "even the dogs under the table eat the children's crumbs." On hearing this, Jesus relented and cured the little girl.[47] In all the

Gospels, this brave mother is the only person who manages to get the better of him in an argument.

Nor do Jews seem to merit love. "Whoever comes to me and does not hate father and mother, wife and children, brothers and sisters – yes, even life itself, cannot be my disciple."[48] Why anyone should hate life has never been satisfactorily explained. In the Pentateuch, Jews are commanded to choose life over death.[49] Indeed the Torah is commonly referred to as a "tree of life" – that is, a guide for living, through which the faithful can give meaning to their own existence and to life itself. The prayer book for Rosh Hashanah, the Jewish New Year, contains the following meditation: "With a father's love, You discipline us, so that we may learn to understand life's holy purpose."[50] In other words, we should all strive, in our own lifetimes, to make the world a better place, however frustrating and time-consuming this may be. But Jesus had other plans. With the kingdom of heaven just around the corner (or so he thought), life in the world as it is did not seem to have any particular meaning.

Only the Nazarene's personal conviction that humanity was about to enter a new, golden age can possibly explain the alacrity with which he sought to abolish the imposing moral edifice that Judaism had built up over the centuries. "Do not judge," he proclaimed, "so that you may not be judged."[51] This is clearly at variance with Jewish teaching. A maxim of Hillel, the great sage who lived some fifty years before Jesus, reads: "Do not judge your fellow human being until you are placed in a situation similar to his."[52] Hillel, a Pharisee, was extremely magnanimous on this question, as on countless others; but he did not reject judgment altogether. In the real world, there are times when judgment is both unavoidable and necessary.

In a similar vein, Jesus told his followers not to resist evil. "You have heard that it was said, 'An eye for an eye and a tooth for a tooth.' But I say to you, do not resist an evildoer. But if anyone strikes you on the right cheek, turn the other also."[53] The commandment to turn the other cheek continues to seduce the unwary. Richard Dawkins, a self-proclaimed "atheist for Jesus," finds it sublime. He claims that Gandhi and Martin Luther King followed this policy.[54] Actually, they did not. Both resisted evil, albeit without recourse to arms. Neither turned the other cheek. Gandhi once confided to his secretary, "We adopted it [non-violence] out of our helplessness. If we had had the atomic bomb, we would have used it against the British."[55] As for Martin Luther King, his courageous speech on 4 April 1967 at the Riverside Church in New York, opposing his country's military engagement in Vietnam, leaves no doubt that he was not passive in the face of injustice. Jesus interpreted "an eye for an eye" to mean vengeance or reprisal, yet he himself vowed reprisal to unbelievers, warning them that "whoever denies me before others, I will also deny before my Father in heaven."[56]

As for turning the other cheek, the saying is not quite as revolutionary as it may sound at first hearing. A passage in the Jewish Scriptures reads: "Let him offer his cheek to one who would smite him. Let him be surfeited with mockery."[57] This particular text refers to young people who need a lesson in humility. For mature adults, however, non-resistance to evil merely makes matters worse by encouraging the evildoer. Its only justification would be to assume, as Jesus apparently did, that universal redemption was imminent. In Judaism, redemption means the triumph of good over evil. If divine providence is about to abolish evil, human resistance might appear to be superfluous.

But what if God does not intervene immediately to set things right, how should we behave? Let us assume that instead of being struck on the cheek, I am hit over the head with a club. Should I ask my assailant (assuming that I am still conscious) to hit me again? In that case, I can die, leaving a widow and two orphans. Or worse: I can survive as a human vegetable, a burden to my family and to society. Judaism has always approved, nay encouraged, legitimate self-defence. One cannot do good to others if one does not exist. To love one's neighbour (or the stranger) as oneself, one first must love oneself.

To justify his doctrine of non-resistance to evil, Jesus set it in opposition to a well-known verse in the Pentateuch: "eye for eye, tooth for tooth."[58] Since then, this commandment has been associated, in the popular imagination, with vengeance or reprisal. It is commonplace nowadays to hear well-meaning people quote the maxim attributed to the great Gandhi, "An-eye-for-an-eye ends in making everybody blind."[59] The *Lex Talionis* first appeared in the Code of Hammurabi and still prevails in certain Islamic countries. In August 2000, an Egyptian living in Saudi Arabia was brought to trial for having thrown acid in the face of a compatriot during a dispute over money. As punishment, he was condemned by the court to have his left eye surgically removed.[60]

No *Lex Talionis* exists in the Hebrew Bible, which specifically forbids vengeance of any kind.[61] "Do not say, 'I will repay evil.' Have faith in the Lord, and He will deliver you."[62] The passage from the book of Exodus has always been understood by the sages of Judaism to be a formula for civil damages following an accident, the financial compensation for the loss of an eye being greater than that of a tooth. The Pharisees stipulated, moreover, that the eye or the tooth of a rich person is worth no more than that of a poor one.[63] In its penal formulation,[64] they interpreted the Biblical verse to mean that all punishment should be proportionate to the crime committed. If the aggressor is himself one-eyed, removing his good eye would make him totally blind.[65] Justice must be tempered with mercy.

Given the true meaning of the Biblical text, as understood by Jews, why did Jesus misinterpret it so flagrantly? Was he acting out of ignorance or did he willfully distort the Torah in order to give emphasis to his own preaching? Whatever his reasons, he succeeded in giving Judaism a bad name – with horrific consequences. Adolf Hitler, among countless others, was influenced by this falsification. In his tragically celebrated speech to the Reichstag on 30 January 1939, he denounced what he called "the vengeful fury of the Old Testament" which supposedly inspires all Jews.[66] Three years later, he cited the Nazarene's egregious distortion of Holy Writ in order to justify a genocide. With a million Jews already murdered, he appeared in triumph before Nazi militants assembled in the Berlin *Sportspalast*. "This time and for the first time," he announced proudly, "the old authentic Jewish law, 'an eye for an eye,' is being applied."[67] Words can kill.

In the Gospels, Jesus sets himself up as being morally superior to Judaism. "You have heard that it was said, 'You shall love your neighbour and hate your enemy.' But I say to you, Love your enemies and pray for those who persecute you."[68] We have already seen that the part about hating one's enemies is pure invention – yet another example of how Jesus misquoted and misrepresented Torah. For the rest, let us take him at his word. To love someone is to stand up for that person and seek to bring him/her joy and happiness. So just how does one go about loving one's enemies? Hitler, for example, liked nothing better than to subjugate the French, enslave the Poles and kill the Jews. To love him, the French would have had to accept subjugation, the Poles, slavery and the Jews, death. In his immortal novel, *1984*, George Orwell shows how the hero, Winston Smith, bravely resists tyranny until he is brainwashed in the Ministry of Love. There, he loses not only his will, but his very identity as a human being. The book ends with the terse phrase: "He loved Big Brother." Although not clinically dead, Smith was, in every other respect, no longer alive. To love one's enemies is to commit suicide.

The Pentateuch contains this telling passage: "I have put before you life and death, blessing and curse.

Choose life – if you and your offspring would live."[69] Yet well-meaning Christians continue to believe that loving one's enemies is the highest form of morality – far superior, in their eyes, to Judaism (about which they know precious little). The Talmud teaches us that the true hero is one who converts an enemy into a friend.[70] This is derived from the Biblical prescription, "You shall not abhor an Edomite, for he is your kinsman. You shall not abhor an Egyptian, for you were a stranger in his land. Children born to them may be admitted into the congregation of the Lord in the third generation."[71] In other words, by patching up differences with people who were formerly unfriendly, you may bring them closer to the Torah. But loving one's enemies without any gesture of reconciliation on their part makes no sense whatsoever.

Let us pursue the Nazarene's reasoning one step further. Should we love those who cause harm to our children? And if we do, how can we possibly love our children? In point of fact, Christians have never loved their enemies, and they are right not to do so. When the Japanese attacked Pearl Harbor on 7 December 1941, the United States government did not send a note to Tokyo inviting the aggressor to bomb San Francisco. Instead, President Roosevelt called on Congress to declare war. His stirring address ended with the rhetorical flourish, "We will gain the inevitable triumph, so help us God!"

Did Jesus love his enemies? Indeed, did he love anyone? He was extremely brusque to his mother at the wedding in Cana[72] (one of the rare occasions on which he deigns to speak with her), and at no time does he show affection or respect for her husband Joseph. Here he is acting true to form, having enjoined his disciples to hate their parents. To some Jews, who had formerly believed in him (i.e. that he was their king) but were beginning to have doubts, he retorted: "You are the sons of your father the devil."[73] This can hardly be called an expression of love, especially since the Jews in question were not his enemies. His malediction had far-reaching effects. For centuries Jews were associated with the devil in popular Christian culture[74] – yet another example of the Nazarene's poisoned legacy.

Jesus reserved his most foul invectives for the Pharisees, as in his all-too-familiar, "Woe unto you, scribes and Pharisees, hypocrites!"[75] Not content with this, he also hurled at them such delicacies as "blind guides,"[76] "serpents" and "brood of vipers," as well as accusing them of being accomplices to murder.[77] These too are hardly expressions of love. They are all the more unjustified since the Pharisees, as we shall see presently, were not his enemies. Not content with this, he called them fools,[78] indeed "blind fools."[79] Earlier, he had warned his disciples that anyone who calls his brother a fool is doomed to the fires of hell.[80] Was this a self-fulfilling prophesy? It is evident, in any case, that Jesus did not practise what he preached.

Notwithstanding these insults, the Pharisees were (and are still) good people. They deserve a fair hearing.

II: Scribes and Pharisees

"Do not think that I have come to abolish the law [*sic*] or the prophets; I have not come to abolish, but to fulfill."[81] Here, Jesus spoke like a true Pharisee. Fulfilling the Torah and the prophetic books of the Bible was exactly what the Pharisees had been doing for generations. For them, fulfilling the Torah meant bringing the blessings of Judaism to all Israelites, even the most humble. The statutes and ordinances of the Pentateuch had to be interpreted so as to allow each and every one to order their lives in a spirit of holiness. Pharisaic Judaism was religious democracy.

It began during the Babylonian exile. Far from the Temple in Jerusalem, the Israelites could no longer offer animal sacrifices, under the aegis of a hereditary priesthood, to atone for their sins or to give thanks for life's blessings.[82] The exiles' penance, like their thanksgiving, came in the form of prayer, which in Hebrew does not mean request, but meditation or soul-searching. The Pharisees referred to prayer as "the sacrifice of the heart." Those who returned to Jerusalem from Babylon engaged in a protracted struggle with the Sadducees, who represented the priestly caste, to have prayers incorporated into the Temple service.[83] The sacrificial cult was retained, but prayers allowed all the faithful to participate in worship.

The Pharisees understood that only by teaching right from wrong could they help the people give meaning to their lives. The source of their doctrine was the Pentateuch, or the five books of Moses. But the Pentateuch is remarkably succinct on many key issues, such as the prohibition of work on the Sabbath.[84] So they asked: what exactly constitutes work? How should the prohibition be applied? They concluded that work involves any physical effort not absolutely necessary to the maintenance of life, whether physical or spiritual. Lifting even a sheet of paper, unless it contains sacred writing, was therefore deemed to be a transgression.

For those unfamiliar with Judaism, this may seem like sterile hair-splitting. But let us see just how this prohibition can – and indeed should – be applied. Imagine a wealthy man feeling thirsty on the Sabbath. So he asks his servant: "As long as you're up, could you get me a glass of water?" This is the thin edge of the wedge which can rip apart the servant's right to weekly repose. If he accedes to his employer's request, he may be called upon to perform other favours, until he finds himself working just as hard as on a weekday.

The Pharisees realized that the weekly prohibition from working was designed primarily to protect those who work, not the leisure class. They themselves were of modest means, small tradesmen and artisans who understood the need for social justice.[85] The Bible prohibits anyone who lives among Israelites, including servants and resident aliens, from working on the Sabbath.[86] So the servant who is called upon to fetch a glass of water, must reply politely: "It is forbidden for me to lift even a sheet of paper. Therefore, I cannot accede to your request." Water is, of course, essential to life. On the Sabbath, the master will have to get his own glass of water and allow the servant his full day of rest.

The servant's rejoinder implies that he is educated in Torah; and to this end, the Pharisees created a network communal institutions known in Hebrew as *Beit-Ha'knesset* (house of assembly) or *Beit-Ha'midrash* (house of teaching), which we know today through their Greek name of synagogue. It was not a temple, since even pagans could attend services. Democratic in spirit, the synagogue can be compared to a center for continuing education in Judaism, a public university for adults.[87] There, people of all social and economic conditions could learn their rights and obligations in Judaism. As a Christian specialist on the Pharisees reminds us, "Torah means teaching. It does not mean Law."[88] The teaching was (and still is) based on casuistry – case law – the study of what should be done in each specific case. Without casuistry, there can be no morality.

Pharisaic Judaism was designed to infuse all aspects of daily life with holiness. It draws its sustenance from what the Pharisees called the oral Torah, those divinely ordained practices that do not appear in the Bible. The written word of God had, of course, been interpreted for generations, but only the Pharisees thought of giving such interpretation legal sanction. To justify the concept of an oral Torah, they invented a charming bit of fiction. Moses, they said, had dictated to scribes the revelation received at Sinai during the daylight hours only. After dusk, he continued to transmit the Torah orally. It was this oral tradition that the Pharisees claimed to be heirs to.

In their pursuit of social justice, the Pharisees often went quite far afield. Typical of their approach is the debate, which opens the *Betsa* tractate of the Jerusalem Talmud as to whether it is permitted to eat an egg laid on the Sabbath or on a religious holiday. At first glance, the discussion seems a frightful waste of time. After all, the hen has to lay an egg every day, and she cannot possible know when Saturday comes around. Many Christian writers have heaped ridicule on the whole idea in order to make Jesus appear superior to the Pharisees.[89] Actually, Jesus never addressed himself to this question; so we cannot possibly know what his position might have been.

These detractors have completely missed the point. We can gain an understanding of what is at issue by noting that the school of Shammai allows one to consume the egg while that of Hillel forbids it. Hillel, who was probably the greatest Pharisee of all time, is noted for his leniency, while Shammai was normally very strict. So why are the roles apparently reversed in this case? The reason is simply this: the Sabbath egg is a symbol for goods produced in violation of laws protecting workers. Nowadays, we would ask: is it permitted to buy an article made in sweatshop conditions, such as a rug woven by small children or a toy made by political prisoners? In light of the debate on eggs, the answer has to be a resounding "No."

The Pharisaic method was never more in evidence than in the interpretation of Leviticus 25, 35-36, which reads as follows:"If your kinsman, being in straits, comes under your authority, and you hold him as though a resident alien, let him live by your side: do not exact from him advance or accrued interest, but fear your God." Here, the Pharisees concentrated their attention on the phrase, "let him live by your side." This is obviously an answer to Cain's question, "Am I my brother's keeper?"[90] But to what extent is one responsible for one's fellow human beings? How far must one go to protect them? So they devised a parable, in which two men undertake to cross a stretch of desert. One brings a flask of water, just sufficient to sustain him throughout the journey; the other brings none. If the former shares his ration with his companion, they will both die, whereas if he keeps it for himself, at least he will survive. What to do?

The sages deliberated arduously over the problem, some claiming that it is better for both to die, rather than having the prescient traveler witness his companion's death. Finally, the majority accepted Rabbi Akiba's position that he should keep the water for himself and save his own life.[91] Judaism has always encouraged self-preservation, rather than senseless martyrdom. To perform *mitzvot* (Hebrew for commandments, but translated freely as acts of loving kindness), one must first exist.

Among the Pharisees' many innovations, the custom of washing one's hands before meals is probably the best known. This practice appears nowhere in the Bible and is not primarily concerned with personal cleanliness.

Rather, it follows the example of the High Priest, who regularly washed his hands in front of the entire congregation before offering a sacrifice. So the most humble of Jews, as he was about to partake of his modest meal, became equal to the High Priest in holiness.[92] To be sure, the Pharisees were not oblivious to questions of hygiene. The evangelist Mark records that, like all Jews, "they do not eat unless they thoroughly wash their hands . . . and they do not eat anything from the market unless they wash it . . . and there are many other traditions that they observe, [such as] the washing of cups, pots and bronze kettles."[93]

Jesus would have none of this. A Pharisee who invited him to dinner was amazed to see that he did not first wash his hands before eating. Jesus returned the hospitality with a stream of insults directed at Pharisees in general, beginning with "You fools!"[94] More abusive language was to follow, especially the all-too-familiar, "Woe unto you, scribes and Pharisees, hypocrites!"[95] Since then, Christianity has spread the pernicious myth of Pharisaic self-righteousness, so that, even today, the very word "pharisee" (lower case) is commonly taken to be a synonym for hypocrite.[96] Nothing, in fact, could be further from the truth. The real Pharisees were the sworn enemies of religious hypocrisy. In the words of Rabbi Simeon, "When you pray, do not consider prayer as a fixed mechanical task, but as an appeal for mercy and grace before the Almighty."[97]

Jesus defended the habit of eating with unwashed hands on both Biblical and hygienic grounds. When the

Pharisees asked him, "Why do your disciples not live according to the tradition of the elders, but eat with defiled hands?" he answered by calling them hypocrites once more and added: "You abandon the commandments of God and hold to human tradition."[98] This is patently absurd: the Pharisees did not abandon a single commandment, since there is nothing in the Torah that forbids washing one's hands before meals. Jesus did not content himself with claiming that washing one's hands before meals could be left to the individual – a purely voluntary act. No, he insisted that it was morally wrong. His opposition to this practice had far-reaching consequences. For centuries, Christians sought to imitate the Saviour by refusing to wash their hands before meals. During the bubonic plague of 1348-1349, the so-called "Black Death," they noticed that fewer Jews were taken ill. Rather than attributing the Jews' relative immunity to personal hygiene, many Christians accused them of poisoning wells. As was only too common in the Middle Ages, persecutions followed.

The Pharisees had good reason to question Jesus on the hand-washing issue. He was supposed to be the King of Israel (or so his followers thought), and the Pharisees had the daunting task of determining if his candidacy was valid. Now that all Jews were enjoined to wash their hands before meals in imitation of the High Priest, it seemed only logical that their king should do the same. If he refused, then perhaps he was not a king after all. Jesus knew that the people would not accept him as their sovereign without the Pharisees' approval. His repeated invectives against them can be explained, in part at least, on political grounds: he apparently realized early in his ministry that their approval might not be forthcoming.

To make matters worse, Jesus claimed that what enters the mouth cannot possibly defile "since it enters, not the heart but the stomach, and goes out into the sewer." The evangelist interprets this phrase to mean that "he declared all foods clean."[99] Here again, Jesus is in error. One does not have to keep kosher to recognize that all foods are not clean and that some, such as certain mushrooms, are highly toxic. The digestive system cannot eliminate all poisons, and touching food with dirty hands contaminates what we eat. So Jesus, who claimed that he had not come to abolish the Torah but to fulfill it, effectively threw the dietary code and personal hygiene out the window.

In yet another dispute with the Pharisees, Jesus unleashed a blasphemy that defies all logic. He claimed that "the son of man is lord of the Sabbath."[100] The expression "son of man" (in Hebrew, *ben-adam*) first appears in the book of Ezekiel and is normally taken to mean any human being, although Jesus may have applied it to himself alone. Whatever interpretation one may choose, the fact remains that in Judaism, only God can be Lord of the Sabbath. The Bible tells that He rested on the seventh day and hallowed it.[101] For observant Jews, the Sabbath is not only a day of rest. It is a time for renewing family ties, for reflecting on the meaning of life and for adding to one's understanding of Torah. As we shall see in chapter V, Jesus did not wish to abolish Judaism or found a church. But when he claimed that one can do whatever one pleases on the Sabbath, he effectively undermined all of Torah, leaving in its place a religion based on his own person.[102] Christianity, once established as a religion, soon adopted most of the Jewish strictures concerning the Sabbath. For centuries, Sunday was deemed to be "the Lord's day," and the faithful were forbidden to engage in their customary weekday activities.

Although a Pharisee himself, Jesus was at odds with the Pharisees on both moral and spiritual grounds. This divergence was duly noted in the early nineteenth century by French scholar Joseph Salvador, who explained that the Pharisees enjoined their coreligionists to partake of life's blessings to the extent that they do not endanger piety. Jesus, by contrast, based his morality on the abnegation of one's basic social necessities. The Pharisees favoured moderation in all things: speech, laughter, sensuality and the quest for riches. They urged their followers to be charitable, to love God and humanity, to seek justice and to commiserate with others in their sorrow. Their moral doctrine, applicable to situations that arise in everyday life, is totally at variance with the absolute morality (loving one's enemies, rejecting worldly goods and family life) put forward by Jesus.[103] To enter the kingdom of heaven, he said, one must first abandon one's domicile, one's spouse and one's children.[104]

As contemporary accounts attest, the Pharisees of Jesus's day were beloved and respected by the great majority of Jews, in Judea as in the Diaspora. They were not a sect, but a community of educators and reformers. The evangelist John, who was no friend of the Jews, rightly acknowledges the Pharisee Nicodemus to be a leader of the people.[105] An unbiased reader of the New Testament cannot fail to be impressed by the Pharisees' remarkable urbanity. Despite the insults showered on them by Jesus, they were invariably polite and never responded in kind. He, by contrast, made no attempt to reason with them or show them where he thought they were in error.[106] They allowed him to preach in their synagogues despite the fact that he had no official status (Judaism was more liberal in those days than it is now). His followers may indeed have called him "rabbi," a Hebrew term which means "my master" or "my teacher," but there was as yet no formal, structured rabbinate. Masters of the Torah made themselves known by reasoned argument; and for a time, the Pharisees gave Jesus the benefit of the doubt.

Of all the encounters between Jesus and the Pharisees in the New Testament, the incident involving a woman taken in adultery is surely the most memorable.[107] The poor creature is portrayed as being surrounded by a group of fanatics, all men, who seemingly want nothing more than to execute her by stoning. It is a tense moment, but Jesus saves her from certain death. First he writes on the ground what Christian tradition holds to be the sins of her accusers. Being of divine origin (or so the story goes), he presumably knew all their sins, right down to the last detail. Then he announces calmly: "Let anyone among you who is without sin be the first to cast a stone at her." Thus challenged, the Pharisees disperse in shame, leaving the woman with her rescuer, who makes her promise not to sin again.

It so happens that this episode does not figure in the original version of John's gospel, or in any other gospel. In view of the literary style, which is markedly different from that of the evangelist, Christian scholars of the New Testament are convinced that the story was inserted by later scribes.[108] They manage to denigrate the Pharisees even more than Jesus's repeated diatribes against them.

Now what are we to make of this fanciful tale? The woman was "taken" in adultery, meaning that she was caught in the act. So where is her lover? The Pentateuch prescribes the death penalty for both parties to an adulterous union, not just one.[109] In Jewish law, a capital offence cannot be adjudicated without the testimony of at least two reliable witnesses. Where are they? The Pharisees, moreover, imposed so many qualifications on penal statutes, especially the death penalty, that it was in fact rarely applied, except in cases of repeated blasphemy, certain forms of incest, and premeditated murder.[110] There is no reason to suppose that they ever intended to have anyone stoned for marital infidelity. If they asked Jesus for his opinion, it was because they were sincerely interested in what he had to say; but they were not obliged to follow his lead on this or any other question.

In this passage the Pharisees are accused of trying to entrap Jesus in order to bring some charge against him. Rather than a trap, the question concerning stoning in general (but without the embellishments in the Gospel) was a test of the Nazarene's moral principles. The Pharisees would not have as their king someone who would apply the death penalty to anything other than the most heinous crimes. His answer, that only someone entirely free from sin may cast the first stone, is in keeping with his earlier pronouncement that no one should ever be judged for anything at all.[111] (This, however, did not prevent him from judging the Pharisees most severely.) The Pharisees took a different position: they held that justice should be tempered with forbearance, but they were not willing to let hardened criminals run free simply because those who sit in judgment might not be totally pure. Jesus apparently believed that, with the kingdom of heaven just around the corner, all sinners and criminals would simply reform themselves. For the Pharisees, justice had to be served in the meantime. Nonetheless, they did not contradict the faith healer from Nazareth. Rather, they simply agreed to disagree.

What they could not abide was Jesus's summary abolition of divorce (Mark and Paul describe this prohibition as absolute; Matthew's gospel allows for divorce only in cases of adultery), along with his refusal to allow a divorced woman to remarry.[112] This is in strict opposition to the Torah, which allows a couple to divorce for any reason and specifies that the divorced woman may marry another man.[113] Earlier, Jesus had said, "For I tell you, until heaven and earth pass away, not one letter, not one stroke of a letter [in the King James Version, "not one jot or tittle"] will pass from the law until all is accomplished."[114] Nothing had, in fact, been accomplished; yet here was Jesus, slashing away at the Torah as if it were of no further importance.

The Pharisees were naturally perturbed at this display of vanity. They did not favour divorce as such, acknowledging it to be a personal tragedy; and they firmly believed that marriages are made in heaven. A charming *midrash*, in this case an anecdote told for pedagogical purposes, relates that a Roman matron once asked Rabbi Yossi ben Halafta: "This God of yours, who created the universe in six days: what has He been doing since then?" The rabbi answered directly: "He has been arranging marriages."[115] But if marriages are made in heaven, they are carried out on earth; and human beings are often fallible. So there has to be a designated exit from a failed marriage.

Jesus antagonized both scribes and Pharisees through his belief in demonology. His powers as a faith healer led him to assume that the sick and infirm were possessed of demons and that, by casting out such evil spirits, he was able to effect miracle cures. He summoned the twelve apostles "and gave them authority over unclean spirits, to cast them out, and to cure every disease and every sickness."[116] Having assumed that all disease was the result of some sin committed earlier, Jesus pronounced his patients, once cured, to be free of sin. On curing a paralytic, he said, "Son, your sins are forgiven." The scribes and Pharisees present were shocked. "Who can forgive sins," they asked, "but God alone?"[117] They were right, since only God knows what sins we have committed. According the C.S. Lewis, Jesus's claim to absolve people of sin proves that he was God.[118] Yet Jesus never claimed to be God (that would have laid him open to the charge of blasphemy); and no one knows, to this day, whether the man did, in fact, receive divine pardon.

The Nazarene replied with a venomous diatribe, accusing his critics of being "full of greed and self-indulgence," ready to murder the prophets. "You snakes, you brood of vipers! How can you escape being sentenced to hell?"[119] This, from the man who had commanded his disciples to love their enemies. Besides, the scribes and Pharisees were not his enemies; they were merely defending Judaism. The scribes had various functions: in addition to Torah scribes, who meticulously copied Holy Writ, there were scribes who taught Torah in the schools; others were notaries and court stenographers. On one of those rare occasions when Jesus quotes Scripture correctly, a scribe praises him.[120]

This not prevent Jesus from singling out the scribes – all of them, without distinction – for his most vicious calumny. Without producing a shred of evidence, he made an outrageous claim: "They devour widows' houses."[121] If this were true, the scribes would be in direct violation of the very Torah to which they were entrusted. It reads in part: "You shall not ill-treat any widow or orphan."[122] Nor should a widow's garment be taken as security for a loan.[123]

Notwithstanding this insult to the scribes, it is the Pharisees who bear the brunt of anti-Jewish propaganda in the New Testament. Luke refers to them as "lovers of money,"[124] an accusation that Jesus himself never made. Contemporary sources indicate that they lived frugally.[125] This particular calumny may have its origin in the bitter rivalry between early Christian missionaries and the

Pharisees, who were active in the dissemination of Judaism not only to pagans, but to Christians as well. Jewish communities in the Diaspora were generally prosperous, so that a prospective convert to Judaism had much to gain materially as well as spiritually. A well-to-do proselyte was welcome in Jewish business circles; a poor one could rely on an extensive network of Jewish charities and welfare agencies.[126] The early church provided neither of these advantages.

The Yom Kippur prayer-book contains a long list of sins for which, if committed, Jews must atone. These include lack of respect for parents and teachers, abuse of power, shady business dealings and one especially suited to Jesus in his strained relationship with the intellectual and moral leaders of Judaism: slander. This particular sin is condemned expressly in the Bible: those who slander may not abide in the tent of the Lord.[127] So to obtain divine pardon, all Jews must first, before the Day of Atonement, seek out those they have offended during the past year and ask to be forgiven. Neither Jesus nor any of the evangelists ever apologized to the scribes and Pharisees.

III: King of Israel?

"Are you the king of the Jews?" Pilate asked Jesus. The latter's response, "Thou sayest"[128] in the King James Version, fails to convey the man's typical effrontery. "So you say" or "That's what you say" would be better translations. Jesus never claimed outright to be the King of Israel; yet he clearly wanted to be recognized as such by his compatriots. His ministry lasted an estimated eighteen months,[129] which is the usual length of a political campaign.

In the course of this campaign, he asked his disciples, "Who do the people ["the multitudes" in some translations] say that I am?" John the Baptist, said one; Elijah, replied another; a resurrected prophet of Biblical times, ventured a third. "But who do you say that I am?" It was Peter who answered: "You are God's anointed!"[130] The word for God's anointed in Greek is *christos*, which most translations render as "the Christ." But neither Jesus nor his disciples spoke Greek; they spoke Aramaic; and they were Jews, not Christians. The word "Christ" would have meant nothing to them, but the Hebrew *mashiach* was familiar to all Jews. It appears thirty-eight times in the

Hebrew Bible and applies to various dignitaries of the house of Israel. A judge is a *mashiach*, as is a prophet, a military leader, the high priest and, of course, the king.[131] Even Cyrus, the King of Persia who allowed the Israelites to leave Babylon for Judea, was given the title of *mashiach*, God's anointed.[132] So we must put Peter's response in its proper context, that of post-biblical Judaism. Anointing with oil was the traditional means by which Israelite kings were consecrated. What Peter said, in effect, was: "You are the King of Israel!" Jesus sternly instructed his disciples not to breathe a word of this to anyone.[133]

And for good reason. To claim kingship in Roman-occupied Judea would have been in itself an open act of rebellion, and Jesus did not want to be prosecuted as a rebel. This accounts for his evasive response to Pilate's interrogation. Throughout his ministry, Jesus remained in Galilee, a region which enjoyed some measure of autonomy from Roman rule. Only at the very end did he venture to preach in Jerusalem. The inhabitants of Galilee were largely uneducated and did not enjoy a favourable reputation among other Jews. In Jesus's day they were often referred to by other Judeans as *am-ha'aretz*, which in Hebrew means literally "people of the land" and is usually rendered in western languages as "peasants." In fact, the term is distinctly pejorative and commonly designates Jews who are ignorant of the Torah. A maxim of the great Hillel states that an *am-ha'aretz* cannot be truly pious.[134] "Hicks" or "yokels" would be a better translation.

These simple folk were especially impressed by the Nazarene's remarkable skills as a faith healer and by his promise that the kingdom of heaven was nigh. The essence of his ministry is described thus: "Jesus went throughout Galilee, teaching in their [the Pharisees'] synagogues, proclaiming the good news of the kingdom and curing every disease and every sickness among the people."[135] The miracle cures convinced many that Jesus was indeed the King-Messiah who would set them free. In Judaism, the kingdom of heaven is taken to mean that God will reign supreme on earth and that, henceforth, everyone will live according to His instruction (i.e. the Torah). Inasmuch as Jews were the only people at the time who actually believed in one God, proclaiming the kingdom of heaven was, in itself, nationalistic.[136]

A less persuasive, but nonetheless important argument in favour of his candidacy to the throne of David was his presumed ancestry. The evangelist Matthew traces his genealogy as far back as Abraham in order to prove that he was of Davidic descent, through Mary's husband Joseph.[137] Actually, the twenty-eight generations from David to Joseph make it virtually impossible to establish such lineage. Luke, after mentioning that Joseph was "of the house of David,"[138] then traces his family tree as far back as Adam – no mean feat.[139] Now we all know, and the evangelists Matthew and Luke make it perfectly clear, that Joseph was not the Nazarene's real, biological father. Jesus never disputed this fact, but he did nothing to dissuade his compatriots that he was of Davidic ancestry. To be chosen King of Israel by popular acclaim it was not absolutely necessary to have David in one's family tree; but it did give the candidate a distinct advantage.

One claim that Jesus never made was that his mother Mary was a virgin. At no point in his ministry did he say: "Now listen up everybody. My mother was a virgin when I was conceived. Therefore I am your king and liberator. So just follow me and ask no further questions." Had he done so, he would have been a laughing-stock among his own people. Whatever their shortcomings, Jews know how babies are made. Previous Kings of Israel had been conceived in the usual way, and the Jewish followers of Jesus did not expect him to be at all different in this regard. In the course of Jewish history, at least thirty-two messianic claimants have either promoted themselves or been put in nomination by their constituents. None ever claimed to have been born of a virgin, and this includes Jesus.[140]

Mary's supposed virginity while pregnant has its origins in Matthew's gospel, which proclaims: "All this took place to fulfill what had been spoken by the Lord through the prophet."[141] And what did the prophet Isaiah say? The passage in the Bible (the "Old Testament" for Christians) to which Matthew alludes has nothing whatsoever to do with the eventual coming of a Messiah. The prophet was asked to give a sign that the King of Judah would soon triumph over his enemies. So he made this prediction: "Assuredly, my Lord will give you a sign of His own accord! Look, the young woman is with child and about to give birth to a son. Let her name him

Immanuel."[142] By the time the boy learns to distinguish good from evil, Judah will be victorious.

In the Hebrew Scriptures, "a sign" applies to an event in the immediate future. It does not refer to something that might take place seven hundred years later. Nor can it, since the young woman is already pregnant. She is most probably the crown princess, the king's daughter. In Hebrew, she is called *ha'almah*, which means the young woman (definite article). An *almah* in Hebrew is a woman of marriageable age, whether a virgin or not. The evangelist, who wrote in Greek, was quoting from the Greek version of the Bible, which renders *almah* as *parthenos*, the classical Greek term for virgin. Yet in Hellenistic Greek, the word *parthenos* no longer applied solely to virgins, but, like the Hebrew *almah*, could mean any nubile young woman.[143]

To accept the virgin-birth story (which also appears in Luke's gospel, but without any reference to Biblical prophesy) as proof positive that Jesus was the Messiah, one has to make two assumptions: first, that the Jews do not know how to read their own Bible (a notion that seems to have originated with Paul, who wrote: "Indeed, to this very day whenever Moses is read, a veil lies over their minds."[144]) and second, that God was playing a cruel trick on them. He seemingly caused Mary to become pregnant by the intervention of the Holy Spirit, but never informed the Jews of this miracle. Actually, the importance of the Holy Spirit in human procreation is an idea straight out of Pharisaic Judaism, which holds that when a man and a woman have sexual relations and truly love one another, the spirit of God is upon them.[145] So to the extent that our parents truly loved one another when we were conceived, we are all children of the Holy Spirit.

Unfortunately, we cannot be certain that Jesus's real biological father ever loved his mother. It seems likely that Mary, an innocent Jewish girl, had been made pregnant by a Roman soldier, who forced himself on her. In the ancient Near East, it was common practice for a girl in Mary's condition to be married to an older man, often a widower. Joseph, being a successful tradesman, could offer her financial security, a happy home life and a respectable place in society. As Jesus grew older, he came to realize that his birthday fell less than nine months after his mother's wedding anniversary. Neighbourhood gossip soon revealed that Joseph was not his real father, and Jesus never knew who his real father was.

The void thus created caused Jesus great anguish and helps to explain his negative attitude to family life. "And call no one on earth your father, for you have but one father – the one in heaven."[146] Does this not apply to him especially? Truly, Jesus should be pitied, not worshipped. Once, while addressing a crowd of people, he was told that his mother and his brothers (actually his half-brothers) wished to speak wth him. He turned them away, saying: "Who is my mother and who are my brothers?" Then, pointing to his disciples, he added: "Here are my mother and my brothers! For whoever does the will of my Father in heaven is my brother and sister and mother."[147]

It was as a faith healer that Jesus first attracted public attention. Jews have long believed that a person whose daily life is guided by moderation and self-discipline will normally enjoy good health. Conversely, they assume that illness is often caused by excess or self-indulgence. It is but a short step from such reasonable principles to the belief that a sick person is somehow possessed of an evil spirit. Since all healing is miraculous in one way or another, the healer can be seen as a miracle-worker, with the ability to expel such demons. Even today, some highly revered Hasidic rabbis are considered to possess healing powers. For them, exorcism is no laughing matter, but a serious obligation to be performed only in the presence of the faithful.

When Jesus began to cast out demons from the bodies of sick people in Galilee, he was continuing a well-established tradition, one that has persisted throughout the centuries. In medieval France and England, some kings were reputed to cure people simply by touching them.[148] So perhaps Jesus was a king after all. The Pharisees, who stood by the masses in their hope for a liberator from Roman rule, were inclined to give him the benefit of the doubt.

They were dismayed, however, by his insistence on performing miracle cures in the synagogue on the Sabbath. The synoptic Gospels leave one with the impression that Judaism forbids any kind of healing on the day of rest. Actually, the Pharisees and their rabbinical successors were quite liberal on this point. Their position was based on the maxim that, to save a life, one may violate any commandment except those forbidding idolatry, adultery (a term which in Hebrew includes all sexual sins, notably incest) and murder. Healing on the Sabbath is therefore permitted when the patient's life is in danger. This criterion too was interpreted liberally. A severe pain, a snake bite, a fever, a fracture or loss of blood were considered sufficient grounds for giving medical attention on the Sabbath. Normally, it is forbidden to prepare food on the Sabbath; meals taken on the day of rest consist of cold dishes prepared in advance before sundown on Friday. This prohibition is relaxed to allow for feeding the sick. But in the case of some chronic ailment which did not immediately threaten the patient's life, treatment would have to wait until the following day.

There were two main reasons for this prohibition. The first was simply to allow the healer (the physician, or whomever) his/her day of rest. Anyone who has ever tried to get in touch with a general practitioner on a weekend well knows how much present-day doctors value their leisure time. There is also a deeper reason for not allowing any but emergency medical care on the Sabbath. Healing is always miraculous to some degree, and the Sabbath is no time for miracles. It is a time for reflection, for meditation on one's own conduct and on what rabbis like to call life's holy purpose. A miracle distracts people from their duty to review their own existence on a weekly basis.

Judaism has always maintained that miracles are no basis for moral teaching. An old Talmudic tale describes a dispute involving three rabbis, one of whom posses extraordinary powers. To prove his point on a particular question, he uproots a carob tree by the sheer force of his own will and projects it three hundred cubits from its original site. His colleagues remain unconvinced. So he causes a stream to run backwards. Still, he fails to gain their assent. Finally, he orders the walls of a schoolhouse to fall and then has them suspended in mid-air. At this point a voice from heaven announces that the rabbi is correct. But other two continue to reject his arguments, insisting that a miracle in itself proves nothing.[149]

Every miracle cure effected by Jesus in the Gospels was for some chronic ailment and could easily have waited until the following day. Nearly all took place in synagogues, in front of the congregation and the leader. In one instance, he cured a man whose hand had withered;[150] in another, a woman who had been bent over for eighteen years was able to stand up straight;[151] in a third, the patient suffered from dropsy.[152] Since these conditions did not require immediate treatment, the leader of the synagogue (there were, as yet, no rabbis in a formal sense) told the people to come and be cured on a weekday, not on the Sabbath.[153] Jesus replied by calling the religious authorities hypocrites and countered with a rhetorical question: if an animal fell into a pit or well on the Sabbath, would you not be morally obligated to save it?[154] As usual, the evangelists give Jesus the last word; the Pharisees are reduced to silence. Yet on closer examination, his comparison is not valid. An animal that falls into a pit or well could die if not rescued promptly. Someone with a withered hand or a bad back can surely wait until after sundown on Saturday to be cured.

So why did Jesus insist on healing the chronically ill on the Sabbath? Simply to advertise his candidacy as

King of Israel, as he himself admitted frankly: "If it is by the finger of God that I cast out demons, then the kingdom of heaven has come to you."[155] He hoped that his gifts as a faith healer would win over the masses. But there was hardly any point in performing miracles on weekdays when nearly everyone was out working in the fields and could not witness them. Jesus needed an audience, and the best place to find one was the synagogue, which was filled to capacity on the Sabbath. Here was obviously the quickest and easiest way to gain a popular following.

What is remarkable here is not that the Pharisees had reservations about Jesus's use of the synagogue to advertise his royal candidacy, but that they tolerated it at all. Why were they so liberal? For one thing, Jesus was an observant Jew (on some matters) and could not be denied access to the house of prayer. A pagan faith healer would have promptly been shown the door, but not a Jewish one. Besides, there was always the possibility that he might be the king so anxiously awaited by the Judean populace. This would explain why the leader of the synagogue, in the aforementioned incident, did not rebuke Jesus personally for performing miracle cures on the Sabbath. The Pharisees of ancient times were not hypocrites, as Jesus claimed, and they treated him with the utmost respect. They were, by any standard, far more flexible, far more tolerant of divergent opinions than medieval and modern rabbis, who closed ranks in order to preserve their flock from that Jewish heresy known as Christianity.

The promise that Judea would soon be liberated from Roman rule and the kingdom of heaven established on earth can be found in a series of beatitudes and admonitions known as the Sermon on the Mount. The evangelist has Jesus climb a mountain to deliver his sermon, apparently to convince readers that here indeed was a new doctrine, which was about to replace the Torah which Moses had received at Mount Sinai. In fact, much of the Sermon on the Mount, and in particular The Lord's Prayer, can be found in traditional Judaism.[156] And it certainly was not delivered from a mountain-top. There were no public-address systems in those days; and if Jesus had spoken from such an altitude, no one down below could have heard him. He probably stood on a slight elevation in order to be seen by the populace. "The Sermon on the Mound" would therefore be more appropriate.

In the context of a Judea yearning to be free from Roman oppression, the Sermon on the Mount is best understood as a campaign speech. (Or perhaps several campaign speeches.The evangelist may have strung together some pronouncements attributed to Jesus and fashioned them into a sermon.) Unlike Christianity, Judaism makes no distinction between the spiritual and the temporal. The King of Israel had both a political and a religious status, as did any pretender to the throne of David. Jesus's listeners understood the Beatitudes as applying to them. It was they – the poor in spirit, the meek, who hunger and thirst for righteousness – who would soon reap their reward. These sayings, which were addressed to Jews only, contain several disparaging references to the goyim. "When you pray, do not heap up empty phrases as the Gentiles do; for they think that they will be heard because of their many words."[157] The Gentiles have other faults as well, said the Nazarene: in particular, they strive after material goods. But he comforted his people with the promise that in the kingdom of heaven, everything will be provided for.[158]

Jesus was at his most nationalistic when he lumped together Gentiles and tax-collectors."For if you love those who love you, what reward do you have? Do not even tax-collectors do the same? And if you greet only your brothers and sisters, what more are you doing than others? Do not even the Gentiles do the same?"[159] In Roman-occupied Judea, tax collectors (or "publicans" in the King James Version) were the object of well-deserved contempt. They were in fact tax farmers, Jews to whom taxes were farmed out by the Roman authorities for a set annual fee. In Luke's gospel, John the Baptist warns them not to collect any more than the prescribed amount.[160] This would indicate that it was common practice for them to exceed it and to extort as much money as possible from their compatriots. Jesus struck a responsive chord among the masses by reviling such individuals. In the kingdom of heaven, no taxes would be payable anywhere.

The messianic ideal in Judaism has its origins in the Babylonian exile. With their kingdom destroyed, the Israelites were worried that God might have abandoned them. The prophet Isaiah exhorted the people to keep faith. "Can a woman forget her baby,/Or disown the child of her womb?"[161] Israel (i.e. the spiritual descendants of Jacob) suffers because the Gentiles, awash in ignorance, superstition and idolatry, do not yet understand its message. "He was wounded because of our sins,/Crushed because of our iniquities."[162] The time will come, however, when all men will recognize that they are brothers, having but one father in heaven."For the Torah shall come forth from Zion,/The word of the Lord from Jerusalem./ Thus He will judge among the nations/And arbitrate for the many peoples,/And they shall beat their swords into plowshares/And their spears into pruning hooks./ Nation shall not take up/Sword against nation;/Nor shall they ever again know war."[163] Once the nations learn to accept the basic principles of Judaism, such as loving the stranger as oneself, they will cease persecuting God's treasured people and share in the blessings of His kingdom. In the end, the messianic age will benefit everyone.

The kingdom of heaven proposed by Jesus was rather more restrictive. Whether non-Jews might be admitted remains a moot point, since Jesus instructed his disciples to go nowhere among the Gentiles when proclaiming the good news.[164] Nor may all Jews gain entry. "For I tell you, unless your righteousness exceeds that of the scribes and Pharisees, you will never enter the kingdom of heaven."[165] How many Jews were more righteous than the scribes and Pharisees? How many Jews understood the Torah better than these scholars and educators? In a further restriction, he announced that anyone with money will be excluded. When a man (presumably Jewish, but not necessarily wealthy) asked him how to attain eternal life, Jesus replied: "Sell what you own, and give the money to the poor."[166] But what if the kingdom of heaven is not established on earth immediately? The man is now flat broke and has no means of sustenance. How can he continue to go about his daily life and provide for his family? If we follow Jesus's line of reasoning to its logical conclusion, the recipients of this largesse are henceforth banned from the kingdom of heaven since they now have money.

The Nazarene's aversion to wealth is carried to extremes in a bizarre parable concerning a rich man and a beggar named Lazarus. The rich man is condemned to hell through no fault of his own, except for being rich. The beggar, who has no particular merit except for being poor, is received in heaven by none other than father Abraham.[167] Yet Abraham, in real life, had not been poor. If only poor people can aspire to paradise, as Jesus implies, the patriarch should not have been there in the first place. Moreover, Jesus himself did not disdain the wealthy. Late in his ministry, he associated freely with tax farmers promised them priority status in the kingdom of heaven.

Jesus gave no money to the poor. When a woman broke an alabaster box containing a rare ointment and poured it on his head, his disciples objected to such waste. The box and its precious contents might have been sold and the proceeds distributed among the poor. This incident illustrates, among other things, the essentially political nature of his ministry. The woman was a constituent. She believed that he was the King of Israel and decided to anoint him herself. Jesus, who could hardly refuse such an honour without offending the woman and losing her political support, answered his disciples, somewhat coldly: "You will always have the poor among you, and you can show them kindness whenever you wish, but you will not always have me."[168] Compare this egotistical declaration to the original admonition in the Pentateuch: "For there will never cease to be needy ones in your land, which is why I command you: open your hand to the poor and needy kinsman in your land."[169] Here, the Israelites are enjoined to practise charity without delay. Jesus, on the other hand, believed that there was no particular urgency in helping the poor. They could wait; he came first.

So to enter the kingdom of heaven, one must be poor and exceed in righteousness the scribes and Pharisees. Yet poor Jews were hardly more righteous than the Scribes and Pharisees, whereas tax farmers and prostitutes, to whom Jesus came to grant special status,[170] were not generally regarded as paragons of virtue. One can only conclude that the kingdom promised by Jesus would be sparsely populated. It is unlikely that Gentiles would gain access. For although Jesus had little use for the scribes and Pharisees, he probably considered them to be morally superior to the *goyim*. In his vew, there is lttle hope for the rich. "Again I tell you, it is easier for a camel to go through the eye of a needle than for someone who is rich to enter the kingdom of God." The evangelist records that his disciples were astounded and asked pointedly: "Then who can be saved?"[171] Who indeed? In this instance, as in others, the disciples were closer to Judaism than their master. A noted passage in the Talmud begins with the question: "Who is rich?" and provides a simple answer: "He who is satisfied with his portion"[172] The disciples saw no reason why anyone satisfied with his portion should be excluded from the kingdom of heaven.

Nor did they welcome his prohibition of divorce. When Jesus held that a man who divorces his wife and marries another woman is guilty of adultery, they remarked simply: "If such is the case of a man with his wife, it is better not to marry." He answered with a touch of condescension: "Not everyone can accept this teaching, but only those to whom it is given." And who might they be? Jesus cites specifically "eunuchs who have made themselves eunuchs for the sake of the kingdom of heaven."[173] Here, he is in total opposition to the Torah, which expressly forbids self-mutilation.[174] Judaism holds that since we have all received the gift of life, we must pass it on to future generations.[175] To castrate oneself is to forego the transmission of life, if not life itself. That Jesus should approve of such extreme (and totally un-Jewish) asceticism is entirely consistent with his rejection of material goods and family ties.

Not everyone who followed Jesus knew of his doctrine. Rather, it was his reputation as a faith healer that made him popular. It had spread throughout Judea and even to neighbouring Syria and beyond the Jordan.[176] During his ministry in Galilee, Jesus performed many other miracles as well. He could walk on water.[177] He could turn water into wine.[178] He multiplied fish[179] and loaves of bread.[180] At one point, he even calmed a storm by the sheer force of his personality. His disciples and the general public were duly impressed.[181] Yet none of these miracles brought the kingdom of heaven any closer.

As long as Jesus limited his ministry to Galilee, he remained relatively safe from arbitrary arrest. The region was not under Roman military occupation; and if the local police tried to apprehend him, there were many Jewish nationalists who would offer him shelter and concealment. To win acceptance as King of Israel, however, he needed a far wider audience, and the best place to find one was in the capital of Judea, Jerusalem. The Passover season, with its message of liberation ("Let my people go."), was fast approaching. Pilgrims from all over the country and the Jewish Diaspora were filling the capital in order to participate in the festivities and offer sacrifices at the Temple. For Jesus, it was now or never; he had no choice but to leave Galilee and make the long journey on foot to Jerusalem.

IV: Jerusalem

As Jesus was leaving for Jerusalem, he encountered a group of Pharisees, who warned him: "Get away from here, for Herod wants to kill you." The Herod in question was Herod Antipas, the son of Herod the Great and tetrarch of Judea. The Roman Empire was ruled largely through tetrarchs, subordinate princelings, whose function was to ensure that the colonized peoples accepted imperial rule. Herod, then, was a satrap of Rome. Naturally, he could not tolerate any challenge to his authority, such as would arise if the people chose someone else as their king. Jesus answered directly, "Go and tell that fox for me: 'Listen, I shall continue to cast out demons and perform cures today and tomorrow, and on the third day . . . I must be on my way'."[182]

The foregoing passage from Luke is remarkable in many respects. It is the only instance in the Gospels in which the Pharisees, as a community, are presented as living, breathing human beings. Elsewhere, they appear merely as straw men, ready to be knocked down by Jesus.

It shows that the Pharisees were not his enemies, constantly looking for ways to trap him, but were genuinely concerned for his safety. They had serious doubts that he was the king who could, by some miracle, prevail over Rome and set his people free. For Jesus relied on miracles. He used his skills as a faith healer to gain a popular following. This is why he insisted in performing more cures before embarking on his fateful journey.

In Jericho, Jesus responded to the pathetic appeal of a blind beggar: "Son of David, have mercy on me!"[183] Here, we see that the Nazarene's reputation as a miracle worker and his presumed Davidic ancestry were powerful drawing cards. Needless to say, the beggar immediately regained his sight. On reaching Jerusalem, Jesus received an enthusiastic welcome from the multitudes lining the highway into town. Some spread their cloaks on the road so that his feet would not touch the ground; others cut branches from the trees. He was acclaimed with the cry: "Hosanna to the Son of David!"[184] A groundswell of popularity bore the faith healer from Nazareth to new heights

Yet even then, his following was beginning to slip away. The citizens of his home town, while acknowledging his remarkable healing powers, refused to recognize him as someone special and indeed "took offence at him,"[185] as well they might, given that he claimed unabashedly: "I am the light of the world"[186] and "I am the way, the truth and the life."[187] The Jews of Nazareth were put off by such egocentricty. Judaism values modesty, as the prophet Micah makes perfectly clear when he tells us what is good and what the Lord requires of us. "It is but to do justly, to love mercy and to walk humbly with your God."[188]

In time, many of Jesus's disciples left him,[189] and even his own brothers did not believe in him (i.e. that he was the King of Israel).[190] The Pharisees, who had been inclined to give him the benefit of the doubt, got tired of being insulted and no longer invited him to dinner. Jesus was poor; indeed he gloried in his poverty. "Consider the lilies of the field, how they grow; they neither toil nor spin. . . . Therefore do not worry, saying, 'What will we eat?' or 'What will we drink?' or 'What will we wear?' For it is the Gentiles who strive for all these things."[191] Nonetheless, he had to eat; and after a time, only tax collectors were willing to offer him and his disciples a free meal. They became his regular hosts at dinner.[192]

A tax collector in Galilee named Levi held a great banquet to which he invited other tax collectors, along with Jesus and his disciples.[193] Levi was obviously a very rich man, having extracted large sums of money from his compatriots. Yet Jesus did not tell him to give all his wealth to the poor in order to enter the kingdom of heaven. On the contrary, in a dispute with the chief priests and elders of the Temple, he answered: "Truly I tell you, the tax collectors and prostitutes will enter the kingdom of God ahead of you."[194] This astonishing statement came from one who, in the Sermon on the Mount not long before, had reviled tax collectors. Now, however, they were his most enthusiastic supporters. The good citizens of Judea held prostitutes in low esteem (as do most people, even today), and they regarded tax collectors as the very dregs of society, comparable to drug traffickers or arms dealers in our own time. But Jesus apparently took no account of their resentment. In the well-known parable of the Pharisee and the publican, he clearly favoured the latter.[195]

The Pharisees were dismayed at Jesus's sudden friendship with tax collectors. "Why do you eat and drink with tax collectors and sinners?" they asked.[196] Their concern was entirely justified, since the tax collectors were the greatest sinners of all: they exploited their own people on behalf of a foreign power. In this, as in other respects, the Pharisees were at one with the masses. Through the synagogue, they exerted a decisive influence over other Jews and won their respect.[197] The more Jesus disparaged the Pharisees, the more his support among his own people declined.

Immediately after entering Jerusalem on Sunday, Jesus repaired to the Temple in order to preach his message that the kingdom of heaven was nigh, but it was already late. So he and the twelve apostles went to Bethany, which is two kilometres or about one and a quarter miles from the centre of town, to spend the night.[198] Why he had to sleep so far away from the Temple has never been adequately explained. Was there no one in all of Jerusalem willing offer temporary lodging to the future King of Israel? Perhaps Jesus was not quite as well-liked as the evangelists make him out to be. On his stopover is Jericho, he had slept at the home of a tax collector, a very rich man who promised to give half (but not all) of his possessions to the poor.[199] Had he accepted another tax collector's hospitality in Jerusalem, he would surely have fallen out of favour with the masses.

As a candidate to the throne of David, Jesus had to win public acclaim."Do not think that I have come to bring peace to the earth," he declared. "I have not come to bring peace, but a sword."[200] The sword metaphor may be taken as a measure of his nationalism. Yet other than Simon Peter, who regularly carried a sword, Jesus had no armed force at his disposal. Just how was he to prevail over the Romans? The verses that follow provide a clue to the Nazarene's relations with the people who, he hoped, would soon choose him as their king. "For I have come to set a man against his father, and a daughter against her mother, and a daughter-in-law against her mother-in-law; and one's foes will be members of one's own household."[201] Jesus had probably read enough of the Bible to know that the messianic age was destined to usher in a general reconciliation of parents and children.[202] His declaration about splitting households was not prophetic, but a simple statement of fact. Whole families were divided as to whether he was indeed the liberator of their nation.[203]

Jesus did make things any easier for his partisans. The elders of the people, both the chief priests and scribes, asked him, "If you are the Messiah, tell us."[204] But he refused to answer. Similarly, he refused to give a sign to the Pharisees that the kingdom of heaven was at hand.[205] They would simply have to accept his prophesy on faith alone. When his own disciples asked him for such a sign, Jesus gave none, predicting instead a period of wars, famine and earthquakes as the birth pangs of the new messianic age.[206] The evangelist does not record their reaction to these dire forebodings, but at one point even Peter denied having any connection with his master.[207]

On Monday morning, Jesus left Bethany to preach the good news in Jerusalem. Apparently his host had not served him a proper breakfast, for he was very hungry. Seeing a fig tree in leaf, he approached it in the hope of finding some fruit; but as the evangelist tells us candidly, "It was not the season for figs."[208] Passover normally falls in April, and fig trees do not bear fruit until late summer. So he cursed the fig tree, which promptly withered to the root and died.[209] In Christian tradition, this incident is regarded as one of the Nazarene's many miracles,[210] but it is vastly different from all the others. Multiplying loaves of bread or turning water into wine enabled the multitudes to eat and drink, but killing a fig tree because it did not bear fruit out of season merely deprived people, especially the poor, of nourishment.

Christian theologians, always ready to give a positive spin to everything Jesus ever said or did, have endeavoured mightily to make some sense out of this bizarre act. Their traditional explanation is that the fig tree represents Judaism and the Jews. "Jewish society," writes one, "is a tree that is vigorous in appearance . . . but it bears no fruit. So it is cursed by Jesus."[211] Such comments are increasingly rare in continental Europe, where the Christian clergy, chastened by the Nazi Holocaust, seek to avoid anything that might encourage anti-Semitism. In English-speaking countries, however, Protestant ministers feel less constrained. An Australian pastor thus summarized a sermon delivered in 2003: "In cursing the fig tree, Jesus prays for God's promised judgment on unbelieving Israel."[212]

Such theological musings raise serious questions. The assertion that Jewish society was sterile during Jesus's lifetime is patently false. In fact, it was probably more dynamic then than it has ever been, before or since. That thousands of Gentiles converted to Judaism every year is ample proof of its vigour.[213] Nor did Judaism wither and die, even after the advent of Christianity. It continued to take in converts, not only among pagans, but also within the newly-formed Christian communities. The anti-Jewish diatribes of the early church fathers, such as John Chrysostom, bishop of Antioch in the fourth century, are proof, *a contrario*, that Judaism remained an influential rival to the daughter religion.[214] The Inquisitor's Manual of the Dominican friar Bernard Gui, which was written in 1307, devotes an entire chapter to the proselytizing activities of what he calls the "perfidious Jews,"[215] thus indicating that the synagogue remained very much alive, even in the shadow of the church.

Since then, Judaism has regained much of its former influence. In the early twentieth century, Aimé Pallière, a French Catholic who discovered Judaism while attending a synagogue service in his native Lyon, noted that "all reforms currently pursued in Christendom are *strictly Jewish* in nature."[216] More recently, two American historians, working from different points of view, have concluded that Jewish thought and culture have permeated all of Western civilization.[217] So if Jesus wanted Judaism to wither away (a doubtful proposition, as we shall see presently), he failed utterly.

The claim that God Himself cursed the Jews and had them punished for not accepting Jesus as their saviour is basically a self-fulfilling prophesy. Having caused Jews to suffer, Christendom took their suffering as proof that God abandoned them long ago.[218] Over the centuries, countless Jews did, in fact, die at the hands of Christians. The Crusades, whose first victims were Jews in the Rhine corridor, the massacres of Jews by Ukrainian Cossacks in 1648, and the Russian pogroms of the late nineteenth and early twentieth centuries were merely a foretaste of Hitler's "Final Solution." To regard these atrocities as God's work is to postulate the existence of a frightfully cruel deity. Did Jesus want most of his coreligionists in Europe (about two-thirds, including a million children under the age of 13) to endure an atrocious death in Nazi extermination camps? If that were so, he would be unworthy of anyone's veneration.

Instead of theological symbolism, we may assume that the fig tree was nothing more than a fig tree and that Jesus, being unable to satisfy his hunger, was in a bad mood. His disciples, who witnessed the incident, made no attempt to interpret it. Furthermore, there is no reason to suppose that their master, on the very first day of his ministry in Jerusalem, sought to curse his own people. On the contrary, he wanted to be accepted as their sovereign. The Australian pastor's reference to "unbelieving Israel" is therefore incorrect. At that moment, Jesus still retained a large popular following. It was only when he realized that his candidacy would be rejected that he turned against most of his compatriots.

So on that Monday morning, Jesus made his way to the Temple. Crowds of Judeans, who were for the most part unlearned in Torah,[219] could hear him preach that the kingdom of heaven was nigh. In the Gospels, we read that Jesus taught *in* the Temple.[220] Actually, he exercised his brief ministry in the outer precincts of the sanctuary, the inner courts being reserved for the priests and Levites. In Galilee, the Pharisees had allowed him to preach in their synagogues; but this was Jerusalem, where the priestly Sadducees dominated. They would not allow someone who was not an official servant of the Temple to announce, within the sanctuary, the coming of a new era in which they would no longer enjoy any special function. Jesus did not seem to mind. In the outer courts could be found throngs of pilgrims from Judea and abroad milling about, buying animals and birds to offer as sacrifices for the Passover holiday.[221] Here was the audience that he so ardently sought.

As Jesus announced the good news, he was approached by the chief priests and the elders of the people, who asked: "Tell us, by what authority are you doing these things?"[222] They had every reason to question him, since the Torah expressly forbids killing a fruit tree under any circumstances.[223] Jesus refused to answer, just as he refused to proclaim himself the Messiah or give a sign that the kingdom of heaven was at hand. The evangelists Matthew and Luke claim that the religious authorities were looking for a way to kill Jesus,[224] but somehow they never managed to pull it off. In John's gospel, he remained in Galilee until Passover because the Jews in Judea had set out to kill him.[225] We may dismiss these accusations since the evangelists, writing several decades after the crucifixion, had no way of reading anyone's thoughts.

In fact, the religious leaders were remarkably civil toward Jesus. Had they wanted to kill him, they would not have asked him if he was the Messiah. Nor would they have approved warmly when Jesus gave as the greatest commandment of all: "Hear, O Israel: the Lord your God, the Lord is one; you shall love the Lord your God with all your heart, with all your mind and with all your strength." Second only to this, he added, was the commandment to love one's neighbour as oneself. A scribe nearby concluded that he was entirely correct.[226] This is not the attitude of someone who wants to kill him. The two commandments can be found in the Pentateuch.[227] Christianity, being trinitarian, has consistently downplayed the first (and more important) of these commandments, which proclaims the unity of God, while attributing the second to Jesus. He was, in fact, a staunch monotheist and would have been at a loss to explain, much less to accept, the trinity.

Jesus lost no time in dissipating his popular following. In John's gospel we read of the anathema he hurled at a group of Jews who had formerly believed in him (i.e. that he was their king) but who were beginning to have some doubts: "You are the sons of your father the devil."[228] Such violent language is hardly an expression of love, and it did not win him any new adherents. It is but one example of the Nazarene's growing wrath at his own people. A Jewish biographer of Jesus, anxious to present him as an exemplary Jew, refuses to believe that such a fine person could possibly have slandered his coreligionists; so he attributes the entire invective to the evangelist. "John's Christ," he writes, "had nothing in common with the real Jesus."[229] (Presumably the apologist knows better than John who "the real Jesus" was.) How simple it all is! All hateful statements and aggressive behaviour attributed to the Nazerene, including those in the Synoptics, are dismissed as mere invention in order to maintain his moral reputation. For if they have any basis at all in fact, then perhaps he was not such a good Jew after all.

Did John really make it all up? For an answer, we must turn to the heated exchange that preceded this outburst. The Jews in question had pointedly reminded Jesus that they, at least, were not conceived out of wedlock.[230] But he was. Jesus never actually claimed to be the biological son of Joseph, but he allowed his followers to believe that, through Mary's husband, he was a direct descendant of King David. If word got round that Joseph was not his real father, Jesus's ambition to be anointed King of Israel would have been severely compromised. In fact, his royal candidacy already stood on a very shaky foundation: few Jews were attracted to his promise of a divine kingdom in which prostitutes and tax farmers would enjoy privileged status.

Worse was to follow. At some point, Jesus flew into a rage and overturned the tables of the merchants and money changers in the Temple forecourt. In Christian tradition, this incident is known as "the cleansing of the Temple," an expression that still has currency. A Protestant theologian who is more familiar with Judaism than most of his colleagues (and who therefore should know better) writes: "The cleansing of the Temple and the cursing of the fig tree must be read together." In his view, the fig tree "symbolizes the Temple."[231] (No Christian apologist, it seems, can see the fig tree as merely a fig tree. It has to be a symbol for something or other.) Yet Jesus cursed the fig tree *before* making his way to the Temple and *before* his encounter with the merchants and money changers. It is highly improbable that he wanted the sanctuary destroyed since it offered him an ideal venue for his preaching.

The Temple did indeed fall to the Romans some four decades later, but Jesus was not their ally. His popular following was strongly nationalistic and would have abandoned him forthwith had he proposed its destruction. The phrase attributed to the Nazarene, "Destroy this Temple and I will raise it up in three days" refers to the temple of his body.[232] (Jesus presumably could foretell his own resurrection.) Nor would he have sought to abolish the sacrificial cult. He was well aware that his mother Mary and her husband Joseph, following the custom of the day, had offered a sacrifice at the Temple to thank God for his birth.[233]

In the event, nothing was "cleansed." Business resumed just as soon as Jesus left, as it had to, so that the Temple service could still function. The merchants were selling animals for sacrifice: cattle, sheep and doves – especially doves, which were all that most pilgrims, including Mary and Joseph, could afford. Only healthy animals and birds could be sacrificed; each was carefully inspected by the religious authorities before being offered for sale. The money changers allowed pilgrims from abroad to change their foreign coin into local currency in order to buy the sacrificial animals. Both performed a useful service to those who had come to Jerusalem for the express purpose of offering a sacrifice. Indeed, without them, the sacrificial cult would have been virtually impossible. Jesus may indeed have called the Temple a den of robbers,[234] but this is not how his fellow Jews saw it. They knew that they were getting fair value. That he fashioned a whip of cords to assault the merchants and money changers[235] served only to antagonize the faithful. The evangelist Matthew tells us further that Jesus "drove out all who were selling and buying."[236] In other words, his fury was not directed solely at the merchants and money changers, but also at ordinary Jews, many of whom had come a great distance to make the pilgrimage. They can hardly have welcomed this development.

The scene, as portrayed in the Gospels, has inspired many. Adolf Hitler, in an early speech to his fellow Nazis, declared: "My feeling as a Christian points me to my Lord and Saviour as a fighter." (Here, Hitler is probably closer to the truth than Ernest Renan, who characterized Jesus as a "gentle dreamer.") "I read the passage which relates how the Lord gathered His strength and made use of the whip to drive the usurers, the vipers and the cheats from the Temple. Today, two thousand years later, I recognize with deep emotion Christ's tremendous fight for this world against the Jewish poison."[237] Even those who do not share Hitler's anti-Semitism tend to regard the Nazarene's outburst as an act of great courage.

Yet the narrative does not quite ring true; something is clearly missing. To begin with, we may safely dismiss the evangelists' assertion that the Temple incident took place on Jesus's first full day in Jerusalem. Chronology was not their strong suit; and if Jesus had begun his brief ministry in the Judean capital by whipping the merchants and money changers, he would have lost most of his popular following immediately. Every time Jesus entered the outer precincts of the Temple to preach, he passed the merchants and money changers. Since he tolerated their presence (and they his) for at least two full days, we may assume that he had no quarrel with them on grounds of principle. Had he attacked them on Monday, the Temple police would have expelled him forthwith and not permitted him to return.

The incident probably occurred on Thursday, the fourth day of his ministry in Jerusalem, as Jesus and the apostles prepared for the Passover holiday. They did not oppose the sacrificial cult as such; indeed, they sought to turn it to their advantage. The candidate to the throne of David was expected to advertise his majesty by offering a sacrifice in front of everyone, and a pigeon was beneath his dignity; only a paschal lamb would do.[238] But since Jesus and the twelve had very little money, buying a whole animal was beyond their means. So they tried to convince the merchants to offer a lamb free of charge to their new king. When the latter refused, preferring coin of the realm to the promise of a heavenly kingdom sometime in the future, Jesus exploded with anger and set upon them. He was arrested by the Temple police for disorderly conduct and interference with worship.

The Nazarene's temper tantrum in the Temple sealed his fate. Deprived of access to the sanctuary, he no longer had a forum in which to announce the good news. As word of the incident spread throughout Jerusalem, his popularity among his own coreligionists went into a free fall. Neither the Jerusalemites nor the pilgrims from the Diaspora could tolerate anyone who would want to desecrate their holy place. The Roman authorities took careful note of this development. They had refrained from arresting Jesus immediately after his triumphal entry into the Judean capital for fear of precipitating a popular revolt. Now that Jesus had lost most of his following, they felt free to take action.

To be sure, the evangelists present an entirely different story, claiming that Jesus was condemned by the Jewish religious elders for blasphemy and then turned over to the Romans to be crucified. John, writing some sixty years after the event, gives a fanciful account of their supposed plea to the Roman governor of Judea, Pontius Pilate: "We have a law, and according to that law he ought to die because he has claimed to be the son of God."[239] In fact, there is no such prohibition in either the Pentateuch or the Talmud. Judaism holds that all human beings are God's children, and it is not clear from the Gospels that Jesus literally claimed to be God's only son. Here, John is obviously trying to discredit the Torah; and in so doing, he implies that the Creator is playing yet another cruel trick on His people. First, He imposes a "law" forbidding anyone to claim divine parentage and then sends His own son to confound those who respect that law. Had Jesus been found guilty of blasphemy, he would have been stoned to death, not crucified. The Jewish leaders did not have to implore Pilate to execute him since they retained jurisdiction in purely religious matters.

The account in Mark's gospel is closer to the truth. After the Temple incident, Jesus was taken to the high priest, who asked him: "Are you the *mashiach*, the Son of the Blessed One?" In the New Testament, as we have seen, the Hebrew *mashiach*, God's anointed, is rendered in Greek as *christos*. In this context, *mashiach* can mean only one thing: the King of Israel. At every anointing of a king, the high priest pronounced him to be the Son of God. Jesus answered, "I am,"[240] the first and only time that he openly claimed for himself the throne of David. The evangelist, whose knowledge of Judaism was scanty, apparently did not understand that the expression, "the Son of God" referred specifically to the king. Mark took it literally. Without actually having witnessed the scene, he has the high priest condemn Jesus for blasphemy. In reality, claiming to be the King of Israel was not blasphemous, but seditious. The high priest had Jesus delivered to the Romans for the crime of sedition.

Further denigrating the Jews and Judaism is the figure of Judas Iscariot, who reportedly betrayed Jesus at the behest of the chief priests and elders for thirty pieces of silver. The betrayal took the form of a kiss, which the said

Judas planted on his master's cheek to identify him.[241] John, alone among the evangelists, portrays Judas as the apostles' treasurer, claiming that he stole regularly from the common purse.[242] Judas cannot have gained much, since Jesus and the twelve were virtually penniless; but the Judas story has given birth to the pernicious notion that all Jews are money-grubbing traitors. From Jerome in the fourth century through Martin Luther in the sixteenth and on to Karl Barth in the twentieth, Christian theologians have equated Judas with the Jewish people as a whole.[243] Alfred Dreyfus, the French army captain falsely accused (and condemned) for selling military secrets to Germany, was regularly called a Judas in the anti-Semitic press.[244] Nazi party historian Walter Frank referred to Judas in depicting the regime's anti-Jewish policies as part of "the historical process in which God and Satan, creation and destruction confront each other in an eternal struggle." Other propagandists in Hitler's service pursued the theme of an apocalyptic clash between Germany and "world Jewry" (as represented by Judas) still further.[245]

In view of this lamentable tradition, the Judas myth should be examined at its source. There was in fact no need to reveal Jesus's identity since he was extremely visible; everyone – the religious authorities, ordinary people, and the Romans – knew who he was. Jesus himself intimated as much. Addressing the Temple police, he said: "Have you come out with swords and clubs as if I were a bandit? When I was with you day after day in the Temple, you did not lay hands on me."[246] So, why "betray" him at all? Indeed, in order to be recognized as King of Israel, Jesus had to make himself known. He was not shy. As for Judas, he was hardly alone in being disloyal. When Jesus was arrested, "all the disciples deserted him and fled." Peter, who had vowed fealty to his master, later denied knowing him.[247]

With the Nazarene's popularity at a low ebb, the Pharisees gave him one last chance to prove himself as David's rightful successor by asking him if the inhabitants of Judea should continue to pay taxes to Rome. They were not out to defend the Temple; they respected it much as the Labour Party in Great Britain respects the monarchy: a symbol of national unity. Their concern was mainly political. The Sadducees, ardent defenders of the priestly caste, had no use for a Messiah; they were content to live under Roman domination. The Pharisees, being close to the people, tended at first to give each and every messianic claimant (there were several in those days) the benefit of the doubt. But they had to be sure they had the right man. The stakes were high. The true King of Israel would surely free his people, but a false pretender would leave all Judea open to Roman repression.[248]

The question was a reasonable one: if Jesus was truly the liberator of his people, no further taxes would be payable to Rome. Indeed, there would probably be no taxes due to anyone in the messianic age, since all the ills of humanity – war, pestilence, famine, poverty, crime etc. – will have disappeared. That the Pharisees questioned Jesus about taxes indicates the political nature of his ministry. They could have raised purely religious issues, such as his egregious distortions of Holy Writ or his extraordinarily pretentious declaration, "No one comes to the Father except through me."[249] They would have been perfectly within their rights to ask him: "And just how did anyone manage to pray before you came along?" Instead, they confined themselves to the tax question, because it was immediately relevant.

Jesus answered by saying, "Render unto Caesar that which is Caesar's and unto God that which is God's"[250] The evangelists record that the Pharisees were utterly amazed by his response and, as is usual in the Gospels, were reduced to silence. This is hardly likely, since his reasoning was perfectly pharisaic. In ordinary circumstances, taxes had to be paid; the Pharisees did not countenance tax evasion. But these were not ordinary circumstances, and the Nazarene's answer was not what one would reasonably expect from the King of Israel. According to Mark and Luke, this was a trick question, designed to entrap Jesus. In reality, he had set his own trap by failing to tell the religious authorities if he was the Messiah and by refusing to give anyone a sign that the kingdom of heaven was at hand. With the future of Judea at stake, the question was pertinent and perfectly valid.

When the masses learned that Jesus had recommended paying taxes to Rome, they realized immediately that he was not their king and liberator. Simply put, he failed to deliver the goods: i.e. liberation from Roman rule. A true national leader would not have favoured paying any further tribute to a foreign occupier of the land. The common people could not accept as their king someone who would perpetuate the occupation and give free reign to the dreaded tax farmers. So they largely abandoned Jesus, who was already barred from preaching anywhere near the Temple for having attacked the merchants and money changers. Deprived of a forum and a broad constituency, the faith healer from Nazareth found himself in a dead end.

So it was the Pharisees who, in the final analysis, revealed Jesus's claim to the throne of David to be without foundation. Jesus reacted to their questioning by exclaiming, "Why are you putting me to the test, you hypocrites?"[251] He knew that he had played his last card and flew into another of his rages by accusing the scribes and Pharisees in general (but not the Sadducees, who were uninterested in freeing Judea) of hypocrisy.[252] But they were not hypocrites simply because he said so, and they had every reason to put him to the test. In so doing, they exposed the fundamental weakness of his case; and without their approval, he had no chance of winning over the Jewish masses. Earlier in his ministry, Jesus had issued the following warning: "Whoever is not with me is against me."[253] Since the Pharisees were no longer willing to give him the benefit of the doubt, he declared them to be his enemies – and he certainly did not love them.

When Jesus was brought before Pilate, he had already lost the support of the common people. The Roman governor was no friend of the Jews. He had antagonized the inhabitants of Jerusalem by restoring Roman standards, bearing the effigy of the emperor, to the city.[254] These were among the "graven images" prohibited in Judaism. Pilate further offended his Jewish subjects by confiscating the entire Temple treasury, to which all the faithful contributed, in order to finance the construction of an aqueduct.[255] Worse, Luke's gospel tells "about the Galileans [Jesus was a Galilean] whose blood Pilate had mingled with their sacrifices."[256] In other words, the Roman governor of Judea was a thief, a tyrant and a murderer. The evangelists, writing decades after the event and anxious to curry favour with Rome, present Pilate as being somehow beholden to his Jewish subjects. Yet if he really had found Jesus innocent of any wrongdoing, as is claimed in the Gospels, why did he flog him personally?[257] The true nature of the Roman occupiers' position regarding Jesus can be seen in the official charge against him, which read: "King of the Jews".[258]

The Jewish masses in Jerusalem, who by now were thoroughly disillusioned with Jesus, did not mind seeing him executed by the Romans. He did retain a core following, including many women, who wept for him as he was being led away to be crucified.[259] They were soon to become the first Christians. But, as Baron has noted, the bulk of the Jews who witnessed his death certainly opposed him.[260] For generations Jewish apologists have tried to convince Christians that neither they nor their forebears were in any way responsible for the crucifixion; and strictly speaking, they are correct. Crucifixion was a Roman penalty (an especially cruel one; the word "excruciating" is derived from it) reserved for sedition. During the two revolts against Rome in 66-70 and 132-135, thousands of Jewish insurgents were crucified.[261] Yet it is equally true that had the Jews of Jerusalem accepted

Jesus as their king, they would have protected him with their lives. None did, not even his dear friends and hosts, the tax farmers, to whom he had promised a special place in the kingdom of heaven.

The true question, therefore, is not whether the Jews of Jerusalem (plus those pilgrims from abroad who might have been present at the scene) were responsible for the Nazarene's death, but whether they were justified in rejecting his candidacy to the throne of David. Clearly, they found him wanting and preferred to see Barabbas released from prison. For them, Barabbas was a real hero, having led an insurrection during which he killed someone (probably a Roman soldier).[262] Jesus may well have admitted, toward the end of his ministry, that his kingdom was "not of this world."[263] His compatriots, however, had to live in the world as it was. They sought genuine, tangible liberation, not a vague promise which could lead to senseless martyrdom.

Indeed Jesus himself did not seek martyrdom. As he breathed his last, he cried out, in Aramaic, quoting Psalm 22: "My God, my God, why have you forsaken me?"[264] He did not expect to die on the cross and hoped to the very last that divine intervention would stay the hand of force. But none came. Jesus would surely have been amazed to learn that he had to die for the sins of humanity. He was taken down from the cross before sundown and given a Jewish burial.[265]

V: From Jesus to Christianity

"And I tell you, you are Peter, and on this rock I will build my church."[266] This declaration, which appears only once in the Gospels, is usually taken to mean that Jesus intended to create a new religion. Even the *Jewish Encyclopedia* lists him as the founder of Christianity. Yet there is a chronological problem here. According to Matthew, Jesus made this statement sometime, probably many months, before leaving for Jerusalem, where he hoped to be chosen King of Israel by popular acclaim. Inasmuch as he sought to win the full support of his compatriots, the last thing he could possibly have wanted to do would be to see them abandon Judaism.

There are linguistic difficulties as well. The pun "Peter-rock" is in Greek, a language that Jesus did not speak and that Peter, a humble fisherman from the Sea of Galilee, did not understand. The "church" that Jesus presumably intended to create is rendered in the New Testament by the term *ekklesia*, which in ancient Greece meant the assembly of free men.[267] In other words, Jesus planned to establish a synagogue. This is a simple procedure, even today: all it takes is ten adult Jewish males (i.e. over the age of 13) who wish to worship together, plus a Torah scroll. Jesus had twelve apostles, representing the twelve tribes of Israel, along with many disciples. Neither a rabbi nor a *hazan* (cantor) is absolutely necessary, and there are still a few synagogues that function quite effectively without them. Since both the rabbi and the cantor are laymen, the priesthood having disappeared with the Temple in the year 70, any Jew well versed in Torah may lead the service. Was Jesus well versed in Torah? Probably not, but his disciples thought he was. They called him "rabbi" (which in Hebrew means my master or my teacher) and accepted his authority.

The synagogue of Jesus was already in being during his lifetime. In Matthew's gospel, the Nazarene advises his followers how to settle disputes. If one member of the congregation (the "church" in the New Testament) feels offended by another, he should take that person aside and try to eliminate the irritant amicably. Should the offender refuse to make amends, both should appear before two or three witnesses, and then before the entire assembly (the "church" again), and if he refuses to accept even the decision of the "church", then he should be expelled. Jesus couched the expulsion in typically graphic terms: "let such a one be to you as a Gentile and a tax-collector."[268] So the "church" founded by Jesus was in fact reserved for deserving Jews. Not even Jewish tax farmers could join.

After the crucifixion, a small minority of Jews continued to believe in Jesus. But they had to overcome serious doubts. After resting on the Jewish Sabbath, they visited his tomb on Sunday and found it empty. The stone had been rolled away and only the linen shroud covering his body remained. It apparently occurred to no one that Roman soldiers, acting on orders from Pilate, might have removed the corpse in order to prevent his grave from becoming a shrine. Instead, they consoled themselves in the belief that he had been resurrected and carried bodily up to heaven.[269]

Resurrection was a Pharisaic notion, born of the Maccabean wars. Ordinary Jews, anguished at seeing their finest young men cut down by pagan warriors, asked the time-honoured question: why do the righteous suffer? The Pharisees reassured them that when the Messiah comes, all Israel, plus the righteous among the *goyim*, will be resurrected for eternal life – not in heaven, but in a world free from injustice.[270] The followers of Jesus, who believed that he was the Messiah, simply applied this prophecy to him and assumed that his resurrection, along with that of all righteous individuals, would follow in short order. In this and in other ways, the first Christians were largely inspired by the Pharisees.

In the absence of their master, the disciples were at first bewildered. "But we had hoped that he was the one who would liberate Israel. Yes, and besides all this, it is now the third day since these things took place."[271] When he did reappear briefly in a vision, they asked him, "Lord, is this the time when you will restore the kingdom to Israel?" Here we see once again that the expectations of his followers were largely nationalistic. Jesus counseled patience, as he had done in the past.[272] Thus fortified in their faith, they "spent much time in the Temple . . .

praising God and having the goodwill of all the people."[273] How all of this sat with the Roman occupiers of Judea is a matter of conjecture, but they could not have been pleased to see any of their Jewish subjects still thirsting for liberation.

The Romans eventually found an influential ally in Saul of Tarsus, a Jew from Asia Minor who was a Roman citizen by birth.[274] We first encounter Saul in Jerusalem when Stephen, the earliest martyr of the church, was arrested by the Sadducees for blasphemy. Stephen accused the Jews – all of them, without exception – of first having opposed Moses and then having murdered Jesus. He was stoned to death, as Saul looked on approvingly.[275] Saul then went to Damascus in order to find other disciples of Jesus and have them brought to Jerusalem for trial. On his way, he saw Jesus in a vision and became convinced that here, indeed, was the Messiah. When he reached Damascus, he "immediately began to proclaim Jesus in the synagogues, saying 'He is the Son of God'. . . All who heard him were amazed and said: 'Is this not the man who persecuted those in Jerusalem who invoked this name? And has he not come here for the purpose of bringing them bound before the chief priests ?'"[276]

The Jews of Damascus might well be amazed, indeed incredulous, and not just because of Saul's past conduct. All Jews in ancient times understood that we are all God's children and that "the Son of God" (definite article) referred specifically to the king. Jesus was already dead, and he had never been anointed.

Saul was a Pharisee. Indeed all Jews in the Diaspora were Pharisees; only in Judea did the Sadducees have any followers (about ten percent of the population, according to reliable estimates), and then only until the destruction of the Temple. So he naturally believed in resurrection, and he relied on this belief to proclaim that the messianic age was imminent. Having learned from followers of Jesus that their master had been spirited up to heaven, he made this the cornerstone of what was soon to become a new religion. "For if the dead are not raised," he wrote later, "then Christ has not been raised. If Christ has not been raised, your faith is futile and you are still in your sins."[277]

In Judaism the resurrection of the dead for eternal life on earth will come to pass only after all forms of injustice have been eliminated. Yet as Saul pursued his mission, none of the righteous had in fact been raised – only Jesus; and one had to take his resurrection on blind faith. The Romans were still in power; injustice still prevailed. Ignorance, superstition and idolatry were everywhere. Some Jews in Judea could still believe that Jesus would soon return to free them of Roman rule, but those in the Diaspora did not seek national liberation. They had to be persuaded that a fundamental, earth-shaking change had taken place in human nature, and most were incredulous. On encountering such doubts among the Jews of Antioch, Saul announced that "we are now turning to the Gentiles."[278] At this point, Saul took on a new identity. He had adopted a new name: Paul, and a new religion: Christianity.

Paul's decision to rely on the Gentiles had far-reaching political consequences. As long as the Jesus cult was primarily a national movement, it remained a threat to Rome, even after the crucifixion. Once it became a religion, the threat largely dissipated. Paul made this perfectly clear in his first epistle, which was addressed to the nascent Christian community of Rome. "Let every person be subject to the governing authorities. For there is no authority except from God, and those that exist ["the powers that be" in the King James Version] have been instituted by God."[279]

The deification of political power, which Christianity has never renounced formally, is totally at variance with Judaism. The psalmist warns us not to put our trust in princes.[280] The government of men is necessary to avoid anarchy, but it is surpassed by the Torah. Thus, the prophetic passage: "Not by might, nor by power, but by my Spirit – said the Lord of Hosts."[281] In the fullness of time, all humanity will be governed by God's holy doctrine. "From out of Zion shall go forth the Torah, and the word of the Lord from Jerusalem."[282] Until then, however, we must remain wary of politicians. "Love work, refuse domination over others, and seek no intimacy with the ruling power," reads one rabbinical maxim.[283] It has its complement in another: "Be guarded in your relations with the ruling power, for those who exercise it draw no one near to them except in their own interests; appearing as friends when it is to their advantage, they do not stand by a man in his hour of need."[284]

Nowadays, most Christians would probably not accept the principle that all political authority has been instituted by God. Did Hitler, Stalin and Kim Jong-un (to mention only a few) derive their power from God? Paul had the relatively benevolent despots of Rome in mind. He might have recalled those tyrants mentioned in the Bible, such as the Pharaoh who had enslaved the Israelites, but in this case he was addressing himself to Romans and did not want to be accused of subversion. Judaism enjoyed official tolerance in much of the Roman Empire; Christians were tolerated only as members of a Jewish sect. Those who had made a clean break with Judaism, or who were never Jews in the first place, exposed themselves for a time to Roman persecution. In the year 64, a great fire devastated Rome. The emperor Nero blamed it on the Christians and organized a full-scale pogrom against them.[285] The evangelists, whose writings began to appear at this time, reacted by reaffirming their loyalty to Rome and by shifting the responsibility for the crucifixion to the Jews.

They could rely on Paul's epistles, which were written in the years 50-51. Some of the most vicious anti-Jewish slander in the New Testament can be found in the first letter he wrote to the Christians of Thessalonica. Here, the apostle claims that "the Jews killed both the Lord Jesus and the prophets. They displease God and are the enemies of all men." Moreover, they prevent Paul and his associates from converting Gentiles to Christianity. "But God's wrath has overtaken them at last."[286] (God's wrath? Is this the benevolent, loving God of the New Testament?) Recent translations of the Christian Scriptures have tried to soften this diatribe by linking the different clauses. Thus the Jews become *those* Jews who displease God and oppose everyone by hindering the activities of Christian missionaries. Yet in the original Greek, each clause is totally independent of the others. The Jews – all of them – are Christ-killers, the deicide people. They displease God and have always displeased Him.[287] And yes, they are also the enemies of all men. John Wesley, the founder of Methodism, drove this last point home when he referred to Jews as the "common enemies of all mankind."[288]

Paul's blanket condemnation of his former coreligionists was revived recently with the release of Mel Gibson's film, *The Passion of the Christ*, which was denounced by Jewish groups as anti-Semitic. Among those who defended the film were Christians who noted that Gibson was simply following the New Testament. In Denver, Colorado, a Protestant minister posted a sign outside his church, which read: "Jews Killed the Lord Jesus," followed by a reference to Paul's epistle and the word, "Settled."[289] A French Catholic, writing in one of his country's most prestigious newspapers, likewise took Gibson's side. The crucifixion, he claimed, was essentially the Jews' fault, "as is confirmed by Saint Paul."[290] Yet Paul did not actually witness the crucifixion. How could he possibly "confirm" anything relating to it?

In the Gospels, the crucifixion is presented as a combined enterprise in which the Romans, who actually governed Judea, acted on orders of the Jews. Pilate is portrayed as being reluctant to having Jesus executed, but he somehow yields to Jewish pressure. In Matthew's gospel, the people cry out in unison, "His blood be upon us and our children." This blood libel is as old as Christianity itself; and throughout history, Jews have suffered grievously for it. Yet Pilate was not altogether passive. He flogged Jesus personally, which seems odd on the part of someone who, just a few minutes earlier, had found no fault with him. His solders spit upon Jesus, put a crown of thorns on his head and mocked him, saying, "Hail, King of the Jews!" They gave him wine mixed with gall to drink and then crucified him.[291] The Roman historian Tacitus relates that Jesus "suffered the extreme penalty duing the reign of Tiberius at the hands of one of our procurators, Pontius Pilatus."[292] So the Jews did not kill him after all.

Well, not quite. Luke introduces a new element toward the end of his narrative. He quotes the Nazarene's followers as recalling "how our chief priests and leaders handed him over to be condemned to death and crucified him."[293] Let us pause for a moment and analyze this curious statement. To whom was Jesus handed over? To the Romans, of course; but since Luke does not want to antagonize them, they are not mentioned at all. If the chief priests and leaders had actually crucified Jesus, they would not have handed him over to anyone for judgment. Peter entertains the same confusion early in his ministry by accusing the Jews of having crucified Jesus, who was "killed by the hands of those outside the law."[294] In other words, he died at the hands of Gentiles. The Jews never crucified anyone.

As the Christian mission developed, so did the accusation of deicide against the Jews. True, the apostles

did not initially exonerate the Gentiles altogether: in a
diatribe directed at the chief priests and elders, Peter and
John mention the *goyim*, along with Pilate, Herod and the
peoples of Israel, who "gathered together against your holy
servant Jesus, whom you anointed."[295] Actually, of course,
the religious leaders of Judea did not anoint Jesus; he was
never recognized officially as King of Israel. Did Peter and
John know how Jesus died? At one point, they accuse the
high priests and elders (just them, not all Jews) of having
crucified him.[296] At another, they claim that he was hanged
on a tree.[297] Peter repeated this accusation some time later.[298]
Score two for lynching and two for crucifixion.

Paul displays a similar ambivalence. He makes
hardly any mention of the Nazarene's doctrine: the
Beatitudes, the instructions to love one's enemies (and hate
one's parents) find no place in his epistles. At most, he is at
one with his master in condemning divorce.[299] The living
Jesus interests him only slightly, if at all.[300] What matters
is the crucifixion, for without it, humanity cannot be saved.
"We proclaim Christ crucified, a stumbling-block to Jews
and foolishness to Gentiles."[301] On the first point, Paul was
entirely correct: ever since God forbade Abraham from
killing his only son, Isaac,[302] Judaism has steadfastly
opposed the sacrifice of any human being. On the second,
he seems to forget that human sacrifice is one of the most
venerable aspects of paganism. By proclaiming a crucified
saviour, who died for the sins of humanity, Paul struck a
sympathetic chord among many Gentiles, who were
accustomed to this form of reasoning. Yet in other passage,
he writes: "Christ redeemed us from the curse of the law by

becoming a curse for us – for it is written, 'Cursed is anyone who hangs on a tree'."[303] Is this how Jesus died?

For Jews, the Torah (mistakenly translated as "the law") is not a curse, but a blessing. By calling it a curse, Paul effectively condemned all of Judaism. Yet he could not make a clean break with the religion of his birth, for he needed the synagogue in order to propagate his new doctrine. As a Jew, he could not preach in a pagan temple. Having decided to address the Gentiles, he found a receptive audience among those who were attracted to the synagogue. His missionary activities in Asia Minor lasted two years, during which time both Jews and Greeks (i.e. those not born to Jewish parents) heard him preach.[304] Among the latter were "devout converts" to Judaism.[305] In addition to full-fledged converts, Paul's audience included "proselytes of the gate," Gentiles who had abjured idolatry but had not formally converted by undergoing circumcision and accepting all the commandments, such as the dietary laws.[306] The expression is derived from the Pentateuch, which grants rest on the Sabbath to "the stranger that is within thy gates."[307] In Biblical times, resident aliens were admitted to the religious assembly of the Israelites.[308] The Pharisees perpetuated this custom by allowing such "God-fearers" to attend, but not to officiate in, synagogue services. By making Judaism known to countless Gentiles, they made Paul's task that much easier; and he availed himself of whatever support he could find. "To the Jews, I became as a Jew," he wrote.[309] Note his words: he became *as* a Jew; he did not become a Jew. Rather, he relied on his Jewish origins in order to gain access to the synagogue, which provided him with an ideal forum. The apostle to the Gentiles was a consummate politician.

By pretending to be faithful to Judaism, Paul benefitted from the warm welcome given him by Jewish communities throughout Asia Minor. One of his first stops was Antioch, where he and his companions attended Sabbath services at the local synagogue. After reading from the Torah and the prophets, the synagogue officials invited them to speak, saying: "Brothers, if you have any word of exhortation for the people, give it."[310] Present-day synagogues are far less hospitable. It is hardly likely that any Jewish traveler who was not a dues-paying member of the community would be invited to preach on the spur of the moment. Judaism in those days was far more liberal than it is today, and Paul accepted the invitation gladly. He launched into a lengthy sermon, announcing that the Messiah had arrived in the person of Jesus, but the Jews of Jerusalem did not understand his message and asked Pilate to have him killed – by stringing him up on a tree.[311] Just why Paul, who elsewhere proclaimed a crucified Christ, spoke here of a hanging, is not explained in the New Testament. Perhaps he, like Peter, invented this bit of fiction in order to incriminate the Jews. Everyone in the Mediterranean basin knew that crucifixion was a Roman punishment.

The congregants were not at all pleased to learn that their coreligionists had caused the death of the Messiah. So when Paul returned to the synagogue the following Sabbath, he ran into fierce opposition.[312] A similar incident occurred in Iconium.[313] At Thessalonica, Paul preached in the synagogue for three successive Sabbaths before being expelled.[314] His ministry in the synagogue of Ephesus, where "he spoke out boldly" in favour of the new doctrine, lasted three months.[315] A well-established network of synagogues in the eastern Mediterranean, which attracted ethnic Jews, converts and interested Gentiles, enabled Paul to lay the foundations for the Christian church. He realized that the success of his mission depended largely on being perceived as a Jew.

But Paul had a personal grievance with Judaism: it made him conscious of sin. "If it had not been for the law [sic], I would not have known sin." As an example, he cited the tenth commandment: You shall not covet. "Sin, seizing an opportunity in the commandment, produced in me all kinds of covetousness."[316] In time, Christianity incorporated the Ten Commandments, along with many other statutes of the Pentateuch, into its doctrine. No religion can reject morality altogether and maintain a following. A recent convert to Catholicism recalled that the Decalogue, which her atheistic parents had always respected, made her receptive to the message of the church.[317] Yet Paul, the true founder of Christianity, rejected the tenth commandment and, for all we know, the other nine as well. Perhaps the prohibition of homicide made him want to commit murder. He could not abide the Torah, of which the Ten Commandments are very much a part.[318]

According to Paul, sin came into the world through Adam: "one man's trespass led to condemnation for all."[319] Here, in embryo, is the doctrine of original sin, which will be developed centuries later by Augustine. It is totally at variance with Judaism, which holds that sin is an individual responsibility – an act, not a state of being. Every individual can follow *ha'yetzer ha'ra* (the inclination to do evil) or *ha'yetzer ha'tov* (the inclination to do good). But as Jews, we do not hold ourselves (or anyone else) to be inveterate sinners. We are not conceived in sin, born in sin, and naturally prone to sin. Therefore, we have no need of a saviour. Adam's act of disobedience is merely the first sin, which sets in motion the entire human experience. It is not a congenital blemish inflicted on everyone at birth. The inclination to do evil can be overcome by living according to the precepts of the Torah; and some day, all of humanity will recognize God's holy doctrine. Until then, we must all strive to improve the human condition, both material and moral. This is the essence of historical monotheism.[320]

"Live by the spirit, I say, and do not gratify the desires of the flesh." First among the works of the flesh is fornication, which Paul abominates. He prefers chastity. "It is well for a man not to touch a woman."[321] This is in direct violation of the divine commandment, issued to all of humanity: "Be fruitful and multiply."[322] But Paul will not be deterred. "To the unmarried and the widows I say that it is well for them to remain single, as I am. But if they cannot contain themselves, they should marry. For it is better to marry than to burn [with lust]."[323] Judaism takes an entirely different approach. Just as it makes no distinction between the spiritual and the temporal, so it does not attempt to separate spiritual and physical love. The Song of Songs, with all its explicit sensuality, was incorporated into the Biblical canon to remind us that these two forms of love are interdependent. As for marriage, it is considered a positive good. "An unmarried man is but half a man," explained one rabbi.[324]

Paul's opposition to circumcision may seem a bit strange, since he was circumcised himself, as was Jesus. Indeed Paul had his disciple, Timothy, circumcised for reasons of convenience. Timothy was born of a Jewish mother and a Gentile father. By having him circumcised, Paul hoped to impress the Jews whom he was trying to convert to his new religion.[325] At the same time, he recognized that the circumcision requirement, imposed on male converts to Judaism, had hindered the Jewish mission. For many "proselytes of the gate," this was a prime obstacle to accepting Judaism in its entirety. So Paul did away with circumcision altogether, along with the rest of what he called "the law," in order to attract adherents to his new doctrine. More than that, he feared – rightly – that pagans who underwent circumcision would remain within Judaism. "Listen! I, Paul, am telling you that if you let yourselves be circumcised, Christ will be of no benefit to you."[326]

In our own time, the benefits of circumcision are slowly beginning to be recognized by the medical profession. The foreskin, which serves no useful purpose, can atrophy, causing pain and even impotence. It can also lead to infection of the penis. Studies show that the incidence of cervical cancer is considerably less among Jewish and Muslim women than among Christians. Circumcised men are at least 50 percent less likely to be infected with AIDS than the uncircumcised.[327] Yet a court in Cologne, Germany ruled on 26 June 2012 that circumcision constitutes bodily harm and may not be performed on infants or young children. A great hue and cry rose up among Jews and Muslims who protested that the right to practise their religion was being violated. Their protests were entirely justified, of course, but the problem goes far deeper. Circumcision is beneficial to all men, and those who oppose it are merely echoing a Christian superstition that has somehow persisted for two millennia.

In Judaism, circumcision is practised on baby boys eight days after birth as a religious obligation which seals the covenant that God made to Abraham. From a purely medical standpoint, this is the best time to perform the operation, since a week-old infant is stronger than at any other moment in the first month of life and can heal rapidly. In an adult man, the healing processes usually lasts a month, during which time the patient must avoid all sexual stimulation. Muslims, who are also descended from Abraham, impose circumcision on boys, but usually delay the procedure until puberty. Jewish tradition, by disconnecting circumcision from sexual development, makes the act itself, like all of Torah, independent of nature.[328] A surgical intervention on a baby boy implies that God did not create a perfect world, but has instead enlisted humanity in its completion.

Completing the world, improving on human nature, will take centuries, even millennia; and Paul was in a frightful hurry. He ranks with those *terribles simplificateurs*, such as Marx and Trotsky, who have lost patience with history and seek a quick fix for all our problems. Faith in the resurrected Christ will, he assumed, absolve all believers of sin. "We will certainly be united with him in a resurrection like his."[329] Paul left no doubt that this glorious occurrence will come quickly. "There is no longer Jew or Greek, there is no longer slave or free, there is no longer male and female; for all of you are one in Christ Jesus."[330] Such distinctions will disappear in the end of time. Until then, wives must be subject to their husbands, and slaves must obey their earthly masters.[331] As for the Jews, they remain the enemies of all men – unlike the Gentiles, who "are a law unto themselves."[332]

In place of the Torah, Paul proposes the doctrine of divine grace, which is said to touch all those who accept Jesus as their saviour.[333] They alone will be washed clean of their sins, a doctrine developed further by Augustine, who ruled that babies who die before baptism will go straight to hell. Augustine's pronouncement was ratified by three church councils – those of Carthage in 418, Lyon in 1274 and Florence in 1438-1445. It remained in force within Catholicism until quite recently. In 2007, Pope Benedict XVI – hardly a radical in theological matters – responded to the anguished cries of Catholic parents whose infants had died before they could be baptized by announcing that there was "hope" for their offspring. Hope, not certainty. This led Reverend Richard McBrien, professor of theology at the University of Notre Dame, to conclude that, in the absence of Augustine's teaching, "we're left with only one option: namely, that everyone is born in a state of grace."[334] In that case, is baptism necessary?

Christianity nonetheless retains a privileged status. According to the New Testament, Christians are "a chosen race, a royal priesthood, a holy nation, God's own people."[335] To this day, most Christian denominations follow the doctrine that Christians are God's elect. It can be found in the catechism of the Roman Catholic Church, which refers to the church (i.e. the assembly of the faithful) as "the people of God," a formula also adopted by Orthodoxy and evangelical Protestantism.[336] Eastern Orthodoxy, to quote one of its spokesmen, "maintains that the church is the people of God and the new Israel."[337]

And what about the "old" Israel? In the Bible (the "Old Testament" for Christians), the spiritual descendants of Jacob are designated as an *am segula*, a people treasured by God. "Now therefore, if you obey My voice and keep My covenant, you shall be My treasured possession among all the peoples."[338] Note that the distinction conferred on the children of Israel depends on their leading a life of holiness. It is not a free gift. The expression "chosen people" appears nowhere in the Hebrew Scriptures but comes from Jerome's Latin translation, the Vulgate. There is, of course, an element of choice here: the Almighty could have given the Torah to all the nations of the earth. Instead, He bestowed it upon the Israelites as a pilot people, who, by teaching and example, are commissioned to lead the nations to a better life, one that is free of sinful behaviour. The Greek Orthodox theologian quoted earlier understands this perfectly by emphasizing that the

Scriptures intend "to draw attention to the universal mission of Israel called by God to promote holiness."[339]

The role assigned to the Israelites confers no privileges, only duties: they must keep the commandments. "The Lord did not set His heart upon you and choose you because you were more numerous than any other people – for you were the fewest of all people."[340] Being few in number, the children of Israel will be rejected and even oppressed by those more powerful than they. God's suffering servant, recalls the prophet, "was despised and rejected by others."[341] But those who hold to the Torah in an idolatrous world should not become discouraged, writes another, for "the righteous live by their faith,"[342] their faith in God's immanent justice (and not, as Paul was to claim later, their faith in a resurrected Christ).[343]

What emerges from the New Testament is a doctrine that is not wholly new and in fact owes much to Judaism. The idea that Christians constitute a royal priesthood is derived from the Hebrew Scriptures and merely confers upon the church a distinction previously reserved for the children of Israel. There remains, however, an important difference between the two forms of election. The Israelites are chosen to serve God; Christians are chosen for individual salvation. Since Judaism does not accept the doctrine of original sin, it does not promise salvation to its adherents. Christianity does, and continues to do so even to the present day.

When Constantine converted to Christianity in 313, it became the official religion of the Roman Empire. No doubt he thought it to be a unifying force in his decaying realm, which was weakened by wars, corruption and the decline of the traditional imperial cult. He could not accept Judaism for reasons other than the circumcision requirement and the dietary laws. Judaism has little regard for those who rule. Paul, on the other hand, proclaimed that all political authority is derived from God. This gave Christianity a distinct advantage, one that favoured its propagation throughout Europe.

That Christianity became the dominant religion of the West is due in no small measure to the Pharisees and their extraordinary magnanimity. Not only did they allow Jesus and Paul to preach in their synagogues; they actually protected the apostles and for many years gave them the benefit of the doubt. When Peter and John appeared before the Sanhedrin and accused its members of having hanged Jesus on a tree, "a Pharisee in the council named Gamaliel, a teacher of the law [sic], respected by all the people" defended their right to speak. After mentioning two messianic candidates who had come to nothing, he declared: "So in the present case, I tell you: keep away from these men and leave them alone; because if this plan or undertaking is of human origin, it will fail; but if it is of God, you cannot overcome it. . . ."[344]

The reference to God was probably inserted by Luke, the author of *Acts*, but there is little doubt that Gamaliel's impassioned plea for tolerance was heeded. Not only were Peter and John released, but all the Jewish followers of Jesus were allowed to remain within the community for at least a century after his death. There was no need to expel them simply they believed in a dead

Messiah who – they hoped – would soon be resurrected to establish the kingdom of heaven on earth. After the destruction of the Temple in the year 70, the priestly caste became redundant and the Sadducees simply disappeared. The Pharisees now dominated all of Judaism and continued to show remarkable forbearance to the Jesus sect.

Calling Gamaliel a Pharisee is like calling the Pope a Catholic. He was in fact the spiritual leader of Pharisaic Judaism, and his followers displayed the same magnanimity to the early Christians. When Paul visited Jerusalem, the Sadducees wanted to kill him, but the Pharisees objected, saying, "We find nothing wrong with this man."[345] The Pharisees prevailed. In Rome, Paul met with the leaders of the local Jewish community, all of whom were Pharisees. They were most receptive: "We would like to hear from you what you think, for with regard to this sect, we know that everywhere it is spoken against."[346] Present-day Christians owe a lot to the much-maligned Pharisees, who allowed Christianity to make its initial impression on the public consciousness. Will they ever recognize this debt?

VI: An Essential Opposition

The words "Old Testament" and "New Testament" have absolutely nothing to do with the document by which people bequeath their worldly goods to their heirs and successors. What they really mean is "old covenant" and "new covenant". Christianity holds that, some two thousand years ago, God found the Jews wanting and summarily dissolved the covenant He had made with them at the foot of Mount Sinai. Henceforth, Christians are God's elect, not merely the "new Israel," but the "true Israel."[347] This is known as the theology of substitution, or supersecessionism. It was reiterated, with ample references to Christian theology, by Pope Pius XII in the encyclical *Mystici Corporis Christi* of 29 June 1943: "On the Cross then the Old Law died, soon to be buried and to be a bearer of death."[348]

The first Christians were blissfully unaware of this dramatic transformation. They continued to observe the Torah – resting on the Jewish Sabbath, following the dietary laws and having their male children circumcised. They differed from other Jews in only one respect: their belief that Jesus was the King of Israel and that he would soon return to establish his kingdom on earth. Paul, whose missionary activities were directed primarily to Gentiles in Asia Minor and the Mediterranean basin, had already broken with Judaism. Within Judea, however, the Jewish followers of Jesus were tolerated by the rabbis as a Jewish sect – one of many – until the second uprising against Rome in 132-135.[349] It was led by Simon Bar Kosiba, renamed Bar Kochba ("son of a star") by the ninety-year-old Rabbi Akiba, who proclaimed him to be the Messiah, the true liberator of Israel. The Nazarites, as the Jewish Christians were then called, could not accept Bar Kochba as the Messiah, since their Messiah, Jesus, had already appeared. None of them would serve in Bar Kochba's army or abjure their faith in Jesus. They were accused of treason, and in particular of revealing Jewish tactics and troop movements to the Romans. As a result, the rabbis of Judea expelled all the Nazarites (in Hebrew: *ha'notzrim*), from Judaism.[350]

Bar Kochba's defeat, coming sixty-five years after the destruction of the Temple, reinforced the Christian belief that the Jews were the object of divine wrath for having rejected Jesus. This pernicious doctrine has its origins in the writings of Paul, that "God's wrath has overtaken them [the Jews] at last."[351] It was reiterated by Martin Luther in his infamous tract, *The Jews and Their Lies*. The destruction of Jerusalem, he claims, is ample proof that the Jews have been displaced by the Christians as God's treasured people. Here, Luther is merely following the New Testament, in which we read that the Jews "stumble, because they disobey the word, as they were destined to do. But you [Christians] are a chosen race, a royal priesthood, a holy nation."[352] This implies that God knew from the outset that the Jews would reject His only son, and that He condemned them to live in perpetual shame.

In the final book of the New Testament, which foretells the Apocalypse, the Jews are singled out for eternal damnation. In fact, they are not Jews at all, since the church has taken their place as the true Israel. They belong to "the synagogue of Satan" because they "say that they are Jews and are not, but are lying."[353] Anyone who types in the words "synagogue of Satan" into a search engine will be flooded with a torrent of anti-Semitic garbage, yet another indication that the New Testament continues to inspire the most vicious hatred of the Jews. The common theme of these entries is that the Jews are the very embodiment of evil and that they control the world. Well, why not? Since they are reputed to be sons of the devil and Christ-killers, they must be more powerful than God Himself. The so-called *Protocols of the Learned Elders of Zion*, the most illustrious (and most dangerous) fake of all time, follows this lamentable tradition.

In recent years, the theology of substitution has encountered serious opposition among Christian theologians and philosophers. It must be embarrassing for them to read a papal encyclical, issued just as the Jews of Rome were being rounded up for the Nazi death camps, which holds the Torah to be a bearer of death. The Nazis, all of whom had been baptized into Christianity, did not observe the Torah. Yet Pius XII was merely echoing Paul, who referred to the role of Moses at Sinai as "the ministry of death."[354] In light of the Holocaust, many established Christian denominations have made valiant efforts to tone down the more egregious anti-Jewish aspects of their religion. The Lutheran Church in the United States issued a statement in April 1994, rejecting the "violent invective" of its founder against the Jews. In November 1998, the Lutheran Church in Bavaria vowed to "distance itself from every [expression of] anti-Judaism in Lutheran theology." Still more encouraging is the discovery by some erudite Christians that Judaism is not totally obsolete, that it has something positive to tell them.[355]

In December 2001, the Pontifical Biblical Commission, presided over by the then Cardinal Joseph Ratzinger, published a pastoral document entitled *The Jewish People and Their Sacred Scriptures in the Christian Bible*.[356] An American member of the Commission hailed it as "a new Catholic approach to Judaism."[357] The real innovation is that the theology of substitution is officially rejected: the church is no longer the "new Israel," but merely the continuation of the old (nuance). For the rest, the document seems designed primarily to assuage the conscience of Catholics. The New Testament, it reads, is not hostile to the Jews. Since few Catholics actually read their holy book, the Vatican's message has a good chance of passing. In order to transmit it, however, the document's authors must take some liberties with the sacred texts of both religions. It is erroneous to assert, for example, that the anti-Jewish calumnies of the New Testament are similar to the denunciations of the Hebrew prophets. Nowhere in the prophetic books of the Bible are the Israelites accused of deicide. As for the Pharisees, they may not be hypocrites (regardless of what Jesus claims), but they are still viewed as legalistic, which in Christian theology seems to be a serious fault.

The progress of the Catholic church in regard to Judaism has been relative at best. During an audience in 2016 Pope Francis accused the Pharisees of not knowing "the heart of God."[358] Presumably he does. After being taken to task by some Jewish scholars (and a few Catholics), the Pope admitted that "for many Jews, the Pharisees are the founders of rabbinical Judaism and, as such, their spiritual ancestors."[359] At bottom, the Pope, like most of his flock, seems to have difficulty understanding Judaism; and it is Jesus who stands in the way. For if we assume that the faith healer from Nazareth is the very paragon of morality, then his calumnies regarding the Pharisees must be well taken. Except that they are not.

Little of the timid measures to absorb the shock of anti-Judaism seems to have trickled down to the clergy at large – in particular the Protestant clergy. A Jewish scholar deeply committed to improving relations with Christians notes with regret that "Christian teaching from the pulpit continues to present a negative picture of Judaism to the faithful, and select readings of New Testament passages confirm the negative impressions." She is especially distressed by the declaration made in 1980 by the Reverend Bailey Smith, president of the Southern Baptist Convention, that "God Almighty does not hear the prayer of a Jew."[360] Here, Reverend Smith is merely echoing Jesus, who said, "No one comes to the Father except through me."[361] For Jews, prayer is not a plea for personal salvation, as it is for Christians. Judaism, following the teaching of the Pharisees, defines prayer as "the sacrifice of the heart" – meditation or self-examination, a perfect example of which is the well-known synagogue text: "May the words of my mouth and the meditation of my heart be acceptable to Thee, O Lord, my rock and my redeemer."[362] When Jews do make a request of God, as in the *Alenu*, it is for an end to war, pestilence and famine, plus the redemption of all humanity from ignorance, superstition and idolatry. This prayer has yet to be answered.

Jewish-Christian dialogue began in earnest shortly after the Second World War. From July 30 to August 5, 1947, a group calling itself the International Conference of Christians and Jews met in the Swiss town of Seelisberg in an effort to reduce, if not to eliminate totally, Christian hatred of the Jews. Of the participants twenty-eight were Jews, twenty-three Protestant and nine Catholic. The Jewish delegation was led by French historian Jules Isaac, whose wife and daughter had been killed by the Nazis, and Jacob Kaplan, the chief rabbi of France. The Catholics present included the Reverend Paul Démann, a convert from Judaism. The conference concluded its proceedings by issuing a statement in ten points, recommending that Christians assume a more tolerant attitude to Jews. In this text, Christians are reminded that Jesus, Mary, the Apostles and the first Christians in Judea were all Jews. Consequently, they should not portray Jews in general as enemies of the saviour. The eighth point is probably the most revealing of the spirit in which the entire statement was adopted. It accepts as "Gospel truth" the blood curse found in Matthew, "His blood be on us and on our children," which all the Jews present at the crucifixion are presumed to have uttered, in unison.[363] This calumny is tempered, however, by a reminder that Jesus said, "Father, forgive them, for they know not what they do."[364]

So the Jews should be forgiven for a crime that they did not commit. In Luke's gospel, Jesus asks God to pardon his tormentors as he is being led away by Roman soldiers to be crucified. Logically, it is they, the Romans, and not his fellow Jews, who should be forgiven. In Judaism, God does not grant pardon unless the sinner atones for his misdeeds. The Jews as a whole never asked forgiveness for having Jesus crucified, for the good and simple reason that it was not done at their behest. By contrast, nearly all Romans (except the Jews of Rome) eventually adopted Christianity. This is surely repentance enough, and it explains why Christians, even today, do not hold the Romans primarily responsible for their saviour's gruesome death.

The Seelisberg conference gave birth l'*Amitié judéo-chrétienne de France*, an association which now has chapters throughout the country. In their preamble to the ten points, the signatories referred to the tragedy that had just befallen the Jews of Europe and called upon the churches of Europe to combat anti-Semitism. Having attended several meetings of this association, the present author can attest to its success in this regard: Jews and Christians in attendance are obviously united in their determination to avoid another Holocaust. For the rest, they pursue vastly different objectives. The Christian participants show a lively interest in the Hebrew Bible, especially the prophetic books. The Jews continue to oppose anti-Semitism, but they seem totally uninterested in learning anything more about Christianity, which in republican France is omnipresent. Major events in the Catholic liturgical calendar, such as All-Saint's Day, Ascension Day and Pentecost, are all national holidays. Catholic churches and cathedrals dominate the urban and rural landscape, while synagogues are largely hidden from public view.

Traditional Jewish indifference to the dominant religion is in part a reaction to the activities of Christian missionaries, who try to ram their beliefs down our throats; it is also a means of insulating Jews from the predominantly Christian culture of Western civilization. In our own day, however, this is no longer possible. Whether they realize it or not, Jews are very much a part of the society in which they live. To ignore Christianity is both archaic and counter-productive. Recently some Jewish scholars, fully committed to their faith, have prepared a voluminous book entitled *The Jewish Annotated New Testament*, in which they explain their endeavours thus: "If we Jews want Christians to respect Judaism, we owe the church the same respect, and that includes knowing what is in the Christian canon."[365] That Jews should read and understand the New Testament is the very premise of this essay, but will such understanding produce respect for Christianity? And should it?

There is an absence of parallelism in the editors' statement: Judaism on the one hand, the church – but not Christianity – on the other. The church is, in its pristine form, the assembly of all the faithful. Individual Christians, most of whom are fundamentally decent people who try to do the right thing, deserve the same respect due to all God's children. But what respect do we Jews owe Christianity? Should we respect a religion whose central figure distorted Holy Writ by claiming that Judaism teaches hatred and encourages vengeance? Should we agree with Jesus that Jews who do not believe in him are sons of the devil? Probably the worst thing that the Nazarene ever did was to slander the scribes and Pharisees. All Jews – or at least all Jews who follow the Torah – are Pharisees. Does that mean that we are all hypocrites? Is this how we want to define ourselves? Does it make any sense to love one's enemies and hate one's parents? Should Jews accept as "Gospel truth" the notion that the blood of Christ must fall on them and on their children?

Anti-Jewish calumnies do not end with the Gospels; they are amplified by Paul and other authors of the New Testament. How can Jews possibly agree with Paul that they are the enemies of all mankind? Is the Jewish house of worship a "synagogue of Satan"? More fundamentally, to respect Christianity is to accept the postulate that God somehow decided to abrogate the covenant He made with the children of Israel. This poses a serious theological problem, which has little to do with the title of *am segula*; it revolves around the question of whether God, having dictated (or at least inspired) the Torah, should, at some point in time, decree that it is obsolete. Can one believe in a deity who changes his doctrine with such reckless abandon? There is a limit to how far Judaism can go to accommodate even the most benevolent Christians in the interest of interfaith dialogue, and that limit has been reached.

It has been reached for Christians as well. In a sign of the times, a French observer notes that *l'Amitié judéo-chrétienne* does not seem to be attracting new members.[366] Christians can respect individual Jews, but they cannot respect Judaism without accepting its continued validity. And if Judaism is still valid, it has no need of a successor. For the Christian clergy, both Catholic and Protestant, the problem is compounded by the steady erosion of their respective communities. At this writing, the fastest-growing religion in the United States is "unaffiliated."[367] In France, which long claimed to be "the eldest daughter of the church," some one thousand Catholics each year ask their local *curé* to have them de-baptized.[368] Quebec, once the jewel in the crown of North American Catholicism, is now a *terre de mission*, a land to be evangelized all over again. So indeed is Catholic Spain, as the Pope made perfectly clear during his visit to that country in 2011. The established Protestant churches continue to lose members. Only the evangelicals, who promise the imminent return of Jesus, seem to be making any gains – but for how long? The late Reverend Jerry Falwell announced that the parousia, the second coming of Christ, would take place in 2009, at the latest.[369] The faithful are very patient, but they cannot be kept waiting forever.

Overworked and underpaid pastors, facing dwindling attendance at weekly church services, try to drum up enthusiasm among the remaining congregants by presenting Jesus as a paragon of virtue. Inevitably, this entails presenting the Jews in a negative light, since they rejected him as their king and continue to ignore the cult that has been built around him. We are dealing here with an essential opposition to Judaism, without which Christianity loses its very *raison d'être*. The German Protestant theologian Karl Barth was disarmingly frank in this regard. "The Jews of the ghetto . . . have nothing to attest to the world but the shadow of the cross of Jesus Christ which falls upon them."[370] After calling the Jewish house of worship "the synagogue of death," he asks: "How can there be room today, according to the will of God, for such a thing as the synagogue?"[371] Barth is clearly baffled and dismayed by the continued existence of Judaism. "It is incomprehensible that Israel in its totality is not yet gathered to the church."[372]

Coming only a few years after the Holocaust, Barth's condemnation of Judaism may seem a bit harsh, but it is entirely in line with traditional Christian teaching. If the fig tree, cursed by Jesus because it did not bear fruit out of season, really does represent Judaism, then all of Judaism is cursed. If the Torah is truly obsolete, then it must be discarded forthwith. If it is not, then the Christian dialectic makes no sense at all. In essence, Barth maintains that Judaism and Christianity cannot coexist forever – and he is right. Unfortunately for him and his theology, the Jews have left the ghetto and now assume their rightful place in Christian society. They enjoy, on average, better health, a higher level of education and a more comfortable standard of living that most Christians. Their presence in the media, universities, cultural and political life far exceeds their numerical importance. They continue to win Nobel prizes in all fields, including literature. If Barth were alive today, he would be appalled to learn that Judaism, which he so blithely consigned to the dustbin of history, is once again taking in proselytes.

The Jewish mission is at least as old as the revelation at Sinai, and probably older. Abraham, whose father is said to have been a maker of idols, appears in the Bible as the earliest convert to monotheism. In the Pentateuch, the Israelites are instructed to observe faithfully the statutes and ordinances transmitted by Moses, "for this will be proof of your wisdom and discernment to other peoples."[373] That the children of Edomites and Egyptians may enter the assembly of the Lord after the third generation[374] attests to the hospitality and dynamism of the early Israelite religion. Judaism continued to attract converts long after the advent of Christianity. In 838 Deacon Bodo, the personal confessor to Emperor Louis the Pious, converted to Judaism and changed his name to Eleazar. According to one scholar, this suggests "a more widespread influence of Jewish proselytism" than is usually assumed.[375] It was not until the Jews of Europe were herded into ghettos in the sixteenth century at the behest of the church that their missionary activities largely ceased.

Nowadays, Christians are converting to Judaism in increasing numbers, not because the rabbinate actively seeks converts (it does not), but because they are attracted to a faith that gives meaning to life on earth instead of promising salvation in the hereafter. They encounter many obstacles, particularly among Orthodox rabbis, and have to endure a pervasive Jewish tribalism, which has been aggravated by centuries of exclusion and persecution. Ethnic Jews tend to be suspicious of the convert, often resorting to the hackneyed jibe, "You don't look Jewish," as if physical appearance were a mark of sincerity. Yet these righteous Gentiles usually persevere and manage to overcome such prejudice. Among the most notable examples is Capers Funnye jr., a close relative of Michelle Obama, the president's wife. Raised as a Methodist, he found Christianity wanting and, after exploring Islam, opted for Judaism. He studied hard and was admitted to the rabbinate in Chicago, where he presides over a largely African-American synagogue. Rabbi Funnye's stated aim is to "open the gates of Judaism" to people of varied ethnic backgrounds.[376] This is entirely consistent with the prophetic ideal, "My house shall be called a house of prayer for all peoples."[377]

As Jewish influence – both religious and secular – continues to increase, Protestant missionaries have redoubled their efforts to convert Jews. They rely primarily on excerpts from the Hebrew Scriptures, which they claim are fulfilled in the New Testament. Thus, Jesus is said to have been born in Bethlehem, David's city; in Luke's gospel, Joseph and Mary move there from Nazareth expressly for their son's birth.[378] Their supposed flight to Egypt is cited as fulfillment of the prophetic verse, "Out of Egypt I have called my son."[379] Yet when we read the original text, it is apparent that the son in question is not

Jesus, but the children of Israel – i.e. the Jewish people. "When Israel was a child, I loved him, and out of Egypt I called my son."[380] This verse, written in the past tense, clearly refers to the liberation of the Israelites from slavery in Egypt. In the book of Exodus, Moses is instructed to tell Pharaoh: "Israel is my firstborn son."[381]

Paul tried to convince the Jews that Jesus was literally the son of God by quoting the psalmist, "You are my son; today I have begotten you."[382] He failed, because they knew that this particular verse was customarily recited at the consecration of every King of Israel.[383] Paul's Gentile audience, being ignorant of this ancient practice, accepted his claim at its face value. Here is proof enough, if proof be needed, that there never has been a Judeo-Christian tradition. If there were such a tradition, Jews and Christians would interpret the Bible in much the same way. But they do not. Christians continue to believe that Jesus was born of a virgin, despite the fact that the original Hebrew text refers to "the young woman."[384] Paul himself never alludes to the virgin birth of Jesus, which seems to have been invented later. The passage in Isaiah concerning the suffering servant of God[385] remains a bone of contention between Judaism and Christianity. Although it was written in the past tense, Christians still believe that it refers to the life of Jesus, some seven hundred years in the future. For Jews, the passage clearly applies to them.

Recently, a Jewish scholar of strict observance has discovered that the concept of a suffering Messiah has not always been foreign to Judaism: several rabbis of the Talmudic and medieval periods expected God's anointed to suffer until the kingdom of heaven is fully established.[386] Their messianic speculations did not, however, apply to Jesus. To be sure, he suffered terribly on the cross, but no more so than the many thousands of Jewish insurgents who were crucified during the two uprisings against Rome. Prior to the crucifixion, Jesus does not seem to have suffered at all, except for being hungry much of the time. Throughout history, the Jewish people have suffered far more, often at the hands of Christians.

The failure of both revolts was instrumental in subduing the Jewish messianic impulse. Yohanan Ben-Zakkai, who had obtained the permission of Roman general Vespasian to establish the first rabbinical academy in the world at Yavneh, advised his pupils: "If you are about to plant a sapling and someone announces the arrival of the Messiah, first plant your sapling and then greet the Messiah."[387] In a familiar Jewish folk tale, the town council of a *shtetl* in Tsarist Russia offers to pay the village idiot, who is otherwise unemployable, one ruble a month to wait outside the main gate and inform everyone of the Messiah's coming. A traveler, seeing him pace up and down in the cold weather, asks him what he is doing.

"I have been assigned by the elders to await the Messiah," he replies.

"And what are you paid for this?"

"One ruble a month."

"That's not much."

"No, but I have job security."

The use of Biblical prophesy to support the claim that Jesus was the Messiah is basically dishonest and reveals an abysmal ignorance of what that prophesy is and what it is not. The prophetic writings include Jeremiah's diatribes against his people for having strayed from the path of righteousness. Micah also refers to "the sins of the house of Israel," but promises that "in the days to come . . . the Torah shall go forth from Zion and the word of the Lord from Jerusalem."[388] The book of Jonah, which is read in the synagogue on Yom Kippur, is not essentially prophetic, but teaches us to respect Gentiles and to do our duty toward God. If the children of Israel keep the faith in spite of adversity, if they observe the commandments and do not yield to the temptation of idolatry, the messianic age will come in due course. But none of the Hebrew prophets ever designated a particular individual as the Messiah.

Of all attempts to bring Jews into the church, the "Jews for Jesus" movement is by far the most fraudulent. Most of its members are not even Jews but evangelical Protestants who masquerade as Jews in so-called "messianic synagogues." Their ministers call themselves rabbis, hold services on Saturday, light Sabbath candles, slip a few Yiddish or Hebrew words into their sermons and pretend that one can be a Jew and still believe in Jesus. In a democracy, Christian missionaries have a perfect right to peddle their goods anywhere (in college campuses, for example) and to anyone, including Jews. But there is such a thing as truth in advertising. A church is not a synagogue, and Jews should be aware that by accepting Jesus as the Messiah, they are in fact adopting a religion that is fundamentally hostile to Judaism. The "Jews for Jesus" routinely baptize new adherents.

The movement was founded in 1973 by a Jew who had converted to Christianity some twenty years earlier and was ordained a Protestant minister. He recognized that Jews in general value their ethnicity; so he reassured them that they could retain their Jewish identity while venerating Jesus. At the same time, he successfully exploited the messianic current now prevalent among many Jews – an outgrowth of the Nazi Holocaust and, still more, of Israel´s surprise victory over three Arab armies in 1967.[389] "Do you long for the Messiah?" he asked in substance. "Well, look no further; he has already arrived!" In this regard, the "Jews for Jesus" share a remarkable affinity with the Lubavitcher Hasidim, who also anxiously await the Messiah. The two groups disagree as to who he might be, but both expect him to appear (in the case of Jesus, to reappear) very soon.

Protestant missionaries claim that they love Jews and want to save us from eternal damnation in the afterlife. The European director of "Jews for Jesus" explained that the organization established an office in Germany "so Jews living there can hear the Gospel and be saved."[390] Saved from hell, that is. But how many Christians still believe in hell? Not many, according to the late Pope John Paul II, who found the growing apathy of his flock extremely disquieting.[391] After all, if hell does not exist, what is there to be saved from? Indeed the very concept of hell was made obsolete by the Nazis. At Auschwitz, Belzek, Sobibor and other death factories, they created a hell on earth that surpassed in horror anything that Christian theology could possibly devise. It goes without saying that converts to Judaism are not afraid of being sent to hell. Ethnic Jews, having seen worse, are not particularly concerned about what might happen to them after death; yet some have shown themselves to be vulnerable to the blandishments of the evangelicals.

The latest tactic of Protestant missionaries has led to the creation, in 1984, of a counter-missionary organization known as "Jews for Judaism." It was founded in Los Angeles by Rabbi Bentzion Kravitz and now has branches in New York, Baltimore, Washington, Toronto, Johannesburg, Melbourne and, most recently, Jerusalem. Rabbi Kravitz, who is of strict observance, aspires to recover as many Jews as possible, whatever their spiritual background, from the clutches of Christian missionaries. He is to be commended for his courage and for his willingness to abandon the traditional Jewish approach of ignoring or cursing Christianity. In the past, pious Jews would spit on the ground when passing a church; some still refer to Jesus as *oto ish* ("that man"), as if his very name were profanity. Rabbi Kravitz has written a 60-page handbook entitled, *The Jewish Response to Missionaries*. It is available online, free of charge, and deserves to be read.[392]

To refute the arguments of Christian missionaries, Rabbi Kravitz employs a method similar to that of Gerald Sigal, whose book he strongly recommends.[393] It consists of examining the so-called "proof texts," those references to the Messiah in the Hebrew Bible, and showing that they do not apply to Jesus. This is fine as far as it goes, but it does not address the problem of the Nazarene's ethics and morality, which even the most lukewarm Christians hold to be vastly superior to Judaism. Christian missionary activity, however reprehensible, is only the tip of the iceberg. Beneath the surface lie the common misconceptions about Judaism that still prevail in Western society. Rabbi Kravitz is entirely correct when he designates Jewish education as a powerful antidote to the influence of missionaries. But what is the state of Jewish education today?

For generations, and especially since the Second World War, Jewish children have not been taught Judaism, but Jewish self-awareness. Remember who you are, they are told. Do not give Hitler a posthumous victory by abandoning your Jewish identity.[394] Alan Dershowitz, professor of criminal law at Harvard and an ardent Zionist, recalls that twelve years in a yeshiva left his head crammed full of details concerning the 613 obligations and prohibitions, wearing a *kippa*, praying three times a day and, most of all, living in a Jewish neighbourhood and having only Jewish friends. Not a word did he hear about the joys inherent in Judaism or its many liberating currents. No wonder, he comments, that so many young Jews think of Judaism as nothing more than "an old man saying no."[395] From the vantage point of Reform Judaism, writer and lecturer Douglas Rushkoff adds: "My Jewish education was terrible. It was about protecting Israel and stemming the tide of intermarriage. But no one explained anything about Judaism, about Torah, or even about social justice."[396]

To encourage self-awareness among their pupils, Jewish educators rely heavily on Zionism. But in Israel itself, Christian missions to the Jews have encountered considerable success. Because the evangelicals now support Israel politically and bring thousands of pilgrims to the Holy Land each year, the Israeli government has relaxed earlier limitations on their proselytizing efforts. Since 1970, Christian missionaries have infiltrated every nook and cranny of Israeli society, including its most cherished institution, the Kibbutz. They do not present themselves as who they are, but come as regular volunteers, always ready to explain their faith to Israeli Jews, in the hope of leading them to Jesus.[397] To counter this activity, "Jews for Judaism" opened an office in Jerusalem in January 2008. A press release issued at that time notes that, "In recent years, the number of Christian missionary groups stationed in Israel has grown to alarming proportions." Some 15,000 so-called "messianic" Jews had established over 130 congregations throughout the country.[398] By 2017, their number was estimated at 20,000.[399]

Clearly, Zionism is not the answer to Jewish alienation. Jeremy Rosen, an Orthodox rabbi who was ordained in Jerusalem, is refreshingly forthright on this question. "Zionism," he writes, "has failed to offer anything other than simple nationalism."[400] The handbook of Rabbi Kravitz ends with the personal accounts of four Jews who were drawn into the "Jews for Jesus" movement and subsequently returned to Judaism. One, named Rachel, was born and educated in Tel Aviv. When she emigrated to the United States at the age of twenty, she was already, in her words, "knowledgeable about Jewish and Israeli life, as well as the Bible stories."[401] The Bible stories, but not Jewish ethics and morality as presented in the Torah. Her education in Israel ("the best possible," in her view) did not shield her from the siren song of Protestant missionaries.

Another testimonial comes from Jerry, who recalls: "I was raised in a Conservative Jewish home, and my parents were Holocaust survivors. As a child, I attended Hebrew school and observed the holiday traditions. I always felt proud of being Jewish, especially after visiting Israel." A visit to Israel reinforced his pride, but taught him little or nothing about Judaism. He too fell victim to the evangelicals. Jerry learned much from his experience. "Remember that most Jewish people don't understand the Bible well enough to make an informed decision."[402] The key word here is "decision." In a democracy, which allows us to choose our way in life, it is not enough to be born into a Jewish milieu. One must decide for oneself to follow the tenets of Judaism. This is a personal commitment which entails understanding not only the Bible, but also the rabbinical commentaries thereon, as well as Jewish philosophy and history.

Even a thorough grounding in Judaism may not be enough, if Jews want to participate fully in society. They will inevitably meet Christians, make friends with them and, in some cases, marry them. Living in a predominantly Christian environment, Jews have every reason to learn about Christianity and its essential opposition to Judaism. This will enable them not only to refute the arguments of missionaries, but also to engage in a meaningful dialogue with their Gentile friends and spouses.

VII: Interfaith Dialogue – At Home

Calvin Coolidge, who succeeded Warren Harding as President of the United States in 1923 and remained in office until 1929, was a man of few words. A sincere Christian, he habitually attended church services every week with his wife. One Sunday, however, she was ill and had to remain in bed. So she urged him to go without her, which he did. On his return she asked him:

"What did the preacher talk about, Calvin?"

"He talked about sin."

"Well, what did he say?"

"He's against it."

Coolidge did not elaborate, but we may assume that his pastor was referring mainly to the sins of the flesh. Ever since Paul put fornication at the very top of his list of sins and declared that it is good for a man not to touch a woman, Christianity has never quite managed to accept human sexuality as anything but a necessary evil. Pre-marital relations are still condemned by fundamentalist Protestants, who propose chastity as a positive good; and the hierarchy of the Catholic church regards so-called "artificial" methods of contraception as a mortal sin in most cases.

Contemporary Judaism takes a more liberal, more realistic, stand on these questions; but it has its own nemesis: assimilation and intermarriage. Jews, who seldom agree on anything, have yet to come up with a common definition of assimilation; but everyone knows what constitutes a mixed marriage, and nearly all rabbis of strict observance are against it. They fear that Judaism will disappear if Jews continue to choose partners outside the community. "Mixed marriages are decimating our ranks," lamented Ismar Schorsch, chancellor of the Jewish Theological Seminary, in a 1994 sermon.[403] Given the frightful loss of Jewish lives under the Nazis, it is perhaps only natural that Jews should be concerned about their numerical importance. Yet the glass may be half-full rather than half-empty. That young people who chose to get married at all in these uncertain times should be a cause for rejoicing. Mixed marriages do not have to result in a demographic decline or in the demise of Judaism. If approached in a positive spirit, they could have precisely the opposite effect.

The rabbinical prohibition of intermarriage is based primarily on a single text in the Pentateuch: "You must not make a covenant with the inhabitants of the land, for they will lust after their gods and invite you, and you will eat of their sacrifices. And when you take wives from among their daughters for your sons, their daughters will lust after their gods and will cause your sons to lust after their gods."[404] On quoting this passage, a French rabbi concludes that "mixed marriages are the first step on the path to betrayal, the first act of abdication."[405] He seems to forget that Moses had taken an Ethiopian woman for his wife – a mixed marriage in more ways than one.[406] Yet Moses remained faithful to the Torah, while the bulk of the Israelites, none of whom had married outside the community, quickly lapsed into idolatry and greatly angered him by worshipping a golden calf.[407]

What emerges from these accounts is that the children of Israel were, at that precise moment, terribly lacking in self-confidence. Generations of slavery had led them to consider Egyptian culture superior to their own, and they could not as yet appreciate the Torah which they had just received. So it is hardly surprising that they were admonished not to marry pagans in the land of Canaan, lest they prostrate themselves before idols once again. By contrast, Moses greatly revered the doctrine that was entrusted to him. He had been raised as an Egyptian prince and was not in awe of paganism. There was never any danger that he might assimilate.

The Biblical injunction against making a covenant with the Canaanites can be justified by the fact that the Israelites were about to occupy a country that was already inhabited by another people. The situation is similar to that of the present State of Israel, which has yet to reach a *modus vivendi* with the Palestinians. Nearly all Diaspora Jews, on the other hand, now live as a religious minority in democratic countries. They are parties to a social contract under which, in return for paying taxes and respecting the law of the land, all citizens – Jews and Gentiles alike – are protected by the state from arbitrary arrest, confiscation of their property and other violations of their civil rights. The social contract is the very basis of democracy and has allowed Jews to attain a level of dignity and prosperity unheard of in ancient or medieval times. So whether they realize it or not, Jews in Western society are effectively bound by covenant to the countries of which they are citizens.

Happily, no one in our time invites the children of Israel to lust after pagan deities or offer sacrifices to them. Today's challenge is of a different nature. Jewish parents want their children to retain their Jewish identity and, at the same time, to make their way in the world. So young Jews are encouraged to attend secular universities, where they inevitably find themselves a minority. This is where lasting friendships and marriage with Gentiles often originate. Intermarriage presents Jews with a twofold challenge: to justify the traditional Jewish rejection of Jesus and to explain the very nature of Judaism. Not all Christian friends and spouses of Jews worship Jesus as a divine being, but most tend to regard him as a role model comparable to Gandhi or Martin Luther King. Since few of them actively seek to convert Jews to Christianity, counter-missionary reasoning based on the analysis of so-called "proof texts" is of little value here. In any case, Jews seldom marry evangelicals; their Gentile spouses are usually of a higher intellectual and cultural level – liberal Protestants or non-observant Catholics. Such people are not likely to be swayed by Biblical references to the Messiah, but by arguments of a moral nature.

They will not get much guidance from the recent spate of books, written by Jewish authors, who try to show how Jewish Jesus was. Of course he was a Jew. What else could he have been? Only Nazis and neo-Nazis depict him as an Aryan.[408] He was, in fact, thoroughly Semitic and spoke Aramaic, like his Jewish mother and his Jewish disciples. To drive this point home, Professor Daniel Boyarin, a Jewish scholar of the New Testament, insists that "Jesus kept kosher."[409] Actually, he had no choice, since the Gospels give no indication that he ever prepared his own food. He ate what was offered to him. Coming from other Jews, it was probably kosher. The reference to the dietary code is simply a reminder that Jesus was, after all, a Jew.

Now, in the latest entry on the subject, an Orthodox rabbi, Shmuley Boteach, goes even further, announcing that Jesus *is* kosher. No, the rabbi is not inviting his fellow Jews to take communion. He simply wants them to accept Jesus as a great Jewish sage, depicting him as "a rabbi . . . deeply learned [in] Jewish holy texts."[410] This is a bit too much. To begin with, calling Jesus a rabbi is an anachronism, since the rabbinate did not exist until Yohanan Ben Zakkai founded a rabbinical academy in the year 80 CE. Furthermore, a learned rabbi does not deliberately misquote and misrepresent the Bible. He does not claim that Judaism teaches hatred; nor does he interpret "an eye for an eye" as promoting vengeance.[411] He does not instruct his disciples to hate their parents, their brothers and sisters – nay even their own lives.[412] He does not slander the scribes and Pharisees, since slander is a grievous sin in Judaism, and all rabbis are heirs to the Pharisaic tradition. Finally, no learned rabbi would ever curse a fig tree simply because it does not bear fruit out of season.[413]

It is always tempting to view Jesus primarily as a Jewish nationalist who sought to free his compatriots from

Roman oppression. To be sure, he skillfully wove nationalistic themes into his discourse as a means of promoting his own candidacy as King of Israel. Yet his own nationalism waned as he drew closer to the dreaded tax farmers who exploited their own people for the benefit of Rome. When he announced that they would enter the kingdom of heaven before anyone else,[414] he lost much of his popular following. It disappeared almost completely when he recommended paying taxes to Caesar.[415] Yes, Jesus was a Jew, but not a very good one. He veered dangerously away from Judaism by claiming that "the son of man is lord of the Sabbath."[416]

The current Jewish infatuation with Jesus – indeed with Christianity – has serious political overtones. "Jews and Christians have so much in common," writes Rabbi Boteach. "We must unite behind our democratic values, defend the embattled State of Israel, and participate in a united front against those have vowed to defeat us." And who might they be? Why the tenants of "radical Islam," of course.[417] In a newspaper interview, Rabbi Boteach revealed his preference for the Christian evangelical right which, in his words, has become "Israel's greatest defender."[418] By recognizing Jesus as a learned rabbi, Jews and Christians can overcome their differences, rally behind the State of Israel and defeat radical Islam. Not all Jews want to make common cause with the evangelicals; but if Rabbi Boteach has his way, they may find themselves engaged in a crusade based on "Judeo-Christian values," a concept dear to him and to some other Jewish luminaries.[419]

It goes without saying that Rabbi Boteach, like his confrere Jonathan Sacks and virtually the entire Jewish establishment, is dead set against marriage between Jews and Christians. "Judaism is in danger," he claims. "Fifty percent of Jewish young people chose to marry outside the faith, assimilating and putting the future survival of our nation [sic] in doubt."[420] There is a strange absence of logic here. If Jewish and Christian values are essentially the same, and if Jews and Christians should unite in their defence, why not let them unite in marriage? In fact there is no such thing as a Judeo-Christian tradition: the values of Judaism and Christianity are radically different. Rabbi Jacob Neusner, probably the greatest Jewish scholar of our time and certainly the leading authority on Jewish-Christian relations, asserts that "Judaism and Christianity form quite different religions with little in common." If Rabbi Boteach sees Jesus as a bridge between Judaism and Christianity, Rabbi Neusner argues that no such bridge exists and declares simply that "there should be none."[421] His point of view receives unsolicited support from Professor Bart D. Ehrman, a noted New Testament scholar, who refers to Christianity as "a distinct, anti-Jewish religion."[422]

So where does this leave intermarried couples? Confused? Well, they should be. On the one hand, Jews who marry Christians are accused of endangering Judaism; their Christian spouses are cast in the role of accomplices. On the other, they are told by some prominent Jewish authorities that Judaism and Christianity are so closely related as to be virtually identical. For the editors of *The*

Jewish Annotated New Testament, not only was Jesus an observant Jew (he wore fringes on his garment[423]), but the entire New Testament is largely inspired by Judaism. Indeed it is, but in what sense and to what end? The authors of the Christian Scriptures use Judaism as a foil to demonstrate the superiority of the new religion. Thus Paul interprets the veil with which Moses covered his face after speaking with God[424] to mean that Jews do not know how to read the Bible and that only belief in Jesus can make them understand its real message.[425]

In their headlong rush to embrace Christianity, some Jewish luminaries overlook a few inconvenient facts. "There is perhaps one feature that constitutes all as members of the Judeo-Christian family," writes Professor Boyarin, "namely appealing to the Hebrew Scriptures as revelation."[426] It is not, however, the same revelation. As we have seen earlier, the Christian interpretation of the Bible differs markedly from the Jewish. Worse, Christian editions of the "Old" Testament do not even respect the proper order of its components: Torah, Prophets and Writings. After the five books of Moses, which remain intact, everything is jumbled so as to emphasize the coming of the Messiah (who is presumably Jesus). This is basically dishonest.

And who might be part of the "Judeo-Christian family"? Pope Pius XII? Karl Barth? Certainly not the great Maimonides, who cursed Jesus the Nazarene in no uncertain terms: "May his bones be ground to dust."[427] Maimonides, the most revered of medieval Jewish sages, was not politically correct, and many present-day Jews will surely feel uncomfortable in the presence of one who had the courage of his convictions. That all Jews should cultivate good relations with individual Christians is beyond dispute. But please, not at the expense of the truth. In the current ecumenical frenzy, the spiritual descendants of Jacob must be careful not to sell their birthright for a plate of lentils.

Jesus – more properly the Jesus myth – remains the chief stumbling block to a Christian understanding of Judaism. This is why the young lady's question to her Jewish suitor, "What do you think of Jesus Christ?"[428] is so relevant. He should be able to give a convincing answer after reading this book, explaining gently to his beloved that Jesus did not invent or even practise love and that his ministry to the people of Judea was essentially political. For their relationship to flourish, however, he will probably have to answer other questions, such as these: "All right, you don't believe in Jesus. So what *do* you believe in? Do you believe in God?"

In Judaism the existence of God is an axiomatic truth, not a belief. Jews are required not so much to believe in God, as to keep His commandments, to perform acts of loving kindness. The prophet Jeremiah asserts that the children of Israel suffer because they "have forsaken Me and have not kept My Torah."[429] To this, a third- or fourth-century rabbi adds: "If only they had forsaken Me and kept My Torah!"[430] Judaism demands action, not belief. Yet belief in God certainly helps if we want to believe in man, in the capacity of all human beings, created in God's image, for moral self-improvement. This is at the heart of what Professor Baron calls historical monotheism.[431] It holds that history has a meaning: namely, that all human beings, once enlightened by God's instruction, will eventually learn how to behave. There is obviously no place in historical monotheism for the doctrine of original sin, for if we are all conceived in sin, born in sin and continue to live sinfully, there is no hope for any of us in this world. In that case, only the crucified Christ can save us.

René Rémond, a leading French historian and traditional Catholic, recognizes that many immediate followers of Jesus, being Jews, regarded him as a "loser" because he failed to liberate Judea. As one deeply committed to Pauline Christianity, however, he is personally more interested in the crucified Christ than in the living Jesus. Rémond is increasingly in the minority, as he himself admits. He bemoans the fact that so many of his compatriots have abandoned Catholicism.[432] Perhaps this is because they are no longer interested in being saved. As life expectancy increases, fewer Christians seek personal salvation in the hereafter, but instead try to give some meaning to their own existence on earth. In this regard, they increasingly have adopted, albeit unconsciously, the Jewish approach to life and its many problems. Being ignorant of Judaism, which they have been taught to regard as "the religion of the Old Testament," they look to Jesus for guidance – not as a loser who endured a horrible death on the cross, but as the living harbinger of a new morality based on love. These are the Gentiles whom Jews in the West are most likely to befriend and, in many cases, to marry. With a few exceptions, they should be receptive to the Jewish message.

That message, simply put, is that life is worth living and should be sanctified, that there is more to human existence than merely satisfying one's appetite for food, drink, sex, money, power etc. Each of us is entrusted with a mission in life, known in Hebrew as *tikkun olam*: to help make the world a better place. In this regard, the contrast with Christianity could hardly be more striking. According to Paul, "when we were baptized in Christ Jesus we were baptized in his death . . . we went into the tomb with him and joined him in death, so that as Christ was raised from the dead . . . we too might live a new life."[433] In Judaism, we do not need a new life. The one we have is good enough, provided that we make the most of it. This is precisely what most newly married couples, whether Jewish, Gentile or mixed, hope to achieve together. They should be given all possible encouragement.

Not much encouragement can be expected, however, from Jewish parents whose child wishes to marry a *goy*. If they do not actually go into mourning, as often happened in the past, they usually voice their opposition to such a match loud and clear. As Rabbi Jeremy Rosen notes: "Often it is the least religious parents, who showed no interest in Judaism, who are the most affected and disturbed."[434] They haven't set much of an example for their offspring, and now they wonder what friends and family will say. A *de facto* union between Jew and Gentile, whether heterosexual or homosexual, rarely incurs such opprobrium from Jewish parents as does a mixed marriage.

A wedding is a social event, and Jewish parents normally want it to be – or at least to appear – Jewish, with a rabbi presiding over the ceremony and heaping platters of gefilte fish for the all guests. At first they try to persuade their child to break off the engagement. If he/she refuses, they often rush off to a rabbi in the hope of having the Gentile partner convert to Judaism.

This is not the way to go, as the Talmud makes perfectly clear. Anyone who wishes to convert out of love for a Jew (or for political advantage or out of fear) is not to be accepted.[435] No one should be pressured into converting to Judaism. There may be some cases in which a Gentile has already begun to study Judaism seriously before meeting his/her Jewish spouse; a conversion prior to marriage is possible. In all others, the mixed couple should be allowed to marry in a civil ceremony. The wedding reception that follows can include lots of gefilte fish.

Once married, the lovebirds should be able to work things out for themselves, depending on their degree of religious commitment and mutual understanding. They may both be totally indifferent to questions of a spiritual nature – in effect parties to an "interfaithless" marriage. For the Jewish partner, a problem arises when the conversation turns to Jesus. Long after Christian atheists and agnostics have abandoned all forms of dogma, they tend to retain a favourable impression of him, one that often prevents them from seeing Judaism in its true light. But if either spouse shows any interest at all in Jewish culture, history or ethics, something positive can result.

The Jewish parents, meanwhile, should welcome their non-Jewish son- or daughter-in-law into the family with open arms. They can find expert guidance, *mutatis mutandis*, in the counter-missionary handbook of Rabbi Kravitz, who counsels patience and understanding, rather than confrontation, in dealing with a young Jew who goes off to join the Jesus freaks.[436] Patience and understanding are even more important in the case of a mixed marriage. The child of Jewish parents has not necessarily left Judaism, whereas his/her Christian spouse can, through teaching and example, eventually be drawn to it. But if the Jewish parents maintain a confrontational attitude, they may drive both newlyweds into the church. In that case, not just one person is lost to Judaism, but two.[437] Since most Jewish parents know little about their own spiritual heritage, they cannot be counted on to educate their child's Gentile spouse in Judaism. The best they can do is to show affection for the newlyweds and respect their choice. Education in Judaism will, in most cases, reside with the Jewish spouse, however ill-prepared he/she may be for the task. With good will on all sides, the mixed couple should be encouraged by the Jewish parents, family, friends and the local rabbi to explore Judaism, its history and belief system, as well as its differences with Christianity.

A good starting point might be the Temple incident, already referred to in these pages, in which Jesus set upon the merchants and money changers, overturning their tables and using a whip of cords to drive them away. Two millennia of Christian tradition have put the merchants and moneychangers in such a bad light that it is exceedingly difficult to do them justice. Franklin D. Roosevelt, who was no anti-Semite, compared Wall Street financiers to the Temple merchants on several occasions, notably in his inaugural address of March 1933.[438] Yet if one wants to understand Judaism, past and present, the merchants and moneychangers must be seen in their proper context: that of a cult in which not only personal atonement for sins, but also thanksgiving (for recovering from an illness, for the birth of a child, etc.) was achieved primarily through animal sacrifice, which Jews in ancient times regarded as a gift to God. Jewish pilgrims considered the purchase of sacrificial animals or birds as being perfectly normal, indeed necessary; those from abroad had to change their foreign currency into local coin in order to pay for them. Within the Temple precincts they would get fair value, since the operations of both the merchants and the moneychangers were closely monitored by the Temple authorities.[439]

After the Temple was destroyed by the Romans in the year 70, animal sacrifices disappeared altogether. They were replaced by prayer, the "sacrifice of the heart" so dear to the Pharisees, who wisely inserted a reference to the sacrificial cult of the Temple into the Yom Kippur service. Thus, they could rightly claim to have inherited the mantle of the hereditary priesthood, just as the synagogue is heir to the Temple. The Pharisees also laid great stress on *mitzvot*, good deeds, in keeping with the prophetic maxim: "For I desire goodness, not sacrifice; obedience to God, rather than burnt-offerings."[440] The Pharisaic method of expounding on the written Torah allowed Judaism to move with the times and adapt to changing circumstances, as it has done to the present day.

As Judaism relied on prayer and good deeds to replace animal sacrifice, Christianity has replaced it with the Eucharist, which is also known as the sacrifice of the Mass. Roman Catholicism and the eastern churches still hold that a miracle occurs when the faithful take communion: the host, or communion wafer, literally becomes the body of Christ. Just as sacrifices were eaten in ancient times by both Jews and pagans, the modern-day Christian is said to eat of the sacrifice made by Jesus himself on the cross. For Protestants, the transformation of the bread and wine into the body and blood of the saviour is considered symbolic. All Christian denominations assume that the Eucharist is derived from the Last Supper, the Passover Seder at which Jesus apparently told the apostles to partake of the *matza*, or unleavened bread, as his body, and of the sacramental wine as his blood.[441] Some New Testament scholars have expressed doubt that Jesus actually gave these instructions, which may have been devised by Paul.[442] John's gospel quotes Jesus as saying, "Those who eat my flesh and drink my blood [without referring to wine] abide in me, and I in them," while he was still in Galilee. Many of his disciples found such teaching "difficult"[443] – and for good reason. In Judaism, the drinking of blood, even that of animals and *a fortiori* that of a human being, is absolutely forbidden.[444]

Christianity holds that the Eucharist is the most exalted form of spiritual expression, since it allows the faithful to be at one with Christ. This leaves the intermarried couple with the following option: on the one hand, a life centred around prayer (i.e. meditation or soul-searching) and good deeds; on the other, religious experience based on a weekly miracle. The choice is theirs to make. If morality rather than personal salvation is uppermost in their minds, they may very well choose Judaism for themselves and their children. To make an enlightened decision, they must divest themselves of the myth that the doctrine of Jesus represents an improvement on the Torah. Then they should be able to see Judaism in all its beauty.

The New Testament presents a grotesque caricature of the Jews and Judaism – the "hypocritical" Pharisees who supposedly forbid healing on the Sabbath; the elders of the Temple who are out to kill Jesus but somehow never manage to succeed; the Jews, "enemies of all men," who refuse salvation through the crucified Christ, etc. But it also contains one verse that is absolutely sublime: "You shall know the truth, and the truth will make you free."[445] Christians and Jews alike have a right to know the truth about Judaism.

Bibliographical Essay

Any attempt to understand Jesus and the religion created in his name must, perforce, begin with the New Testament. The reader should bear in mind that the New Testament, as its name implies, is a work of theology which proposes a new covenant, in which the Jews are replaced by the church as the people of God. Henceforth, the old covenant is declared obsolete, and those who still cling to it are at the very least in error, if not actually under a divine curse. Christianity is the only religion in history whose very *raison d'être* is to replace another. It claims to be the heir to Judaism. One inherits from the dead and not the living. Therefore, Judaism must be dead. A spiritual genocide, minutely developed and elaborated upon by Christian theologians throughout the ages, was followed in the twentieth century by a physical genocide. It is in this spirit that the New Testament should be read.

To understand fully the Christian scriptures, they should be studied in the context of Judaism, and in particular that of a Judea chafing under Roman domination. The most successful attempt in this regard is that of Francis Weill, *Juifs et chrétiens, requiem pour un divorce* (Paris: L'Harmattan, 2001). The author explains that the followers of Jesus were not looking for a celestial guide who would save the world from sin, but for "a powerful King of Israel, independent of foreign tutelage" (p. 199). He adds that Jews cannot accept the Christian Jesus, the second person of the Trinity, who is said to have brought forth the messianic age more than two millennia ago (p. 411). Dr. Weill is a physician, not a rabbi. His Jewish erudition is all the more remarkable.

If the New Testament were to be published for the first time today, Jews everywhere would want to have it banned as hate literature; but two millennia as Christianity's holy book have rendered it virtually unassailable. So when Jews, for the most part rabbis, comment on the New Testament, they usually make a special effort not to offend Christians. They limit themselves to philological and literary criticism, emphasizing its many inconsistencies and contradictions; but they studiously avoid making any moral judgments. Samuel Sandmel, in his pioneering work entitled *A Jewish Understanding of the New Testament* (Cincinatti, OH: Hebrew Union College Press, 1956) seeks to impart "a better understanding of Christianity" to his fellow Jews. He regrets "the direct or oblique attacks on Jews and on Judaism" in the Christian Scriptures, but does not mention the accusation against the Jews as sons of the devil or the "synagogue of Satan." Many Christians, he writes (p. 204), understand that "the anti-Jewish tone of the New Testament is the product of an age and of a set of conditions." The message here is that Jews should no longer fear Christianity. But should they refute its claims? Rabbi Sandmel does not say.

In a similar vein, Rabbi Michael J. Cook has written a book whose purpose is explained in its title: *Modern Jews Engage the New Testament: Enhancing Jewish Well-Being in a Christian Environment* (Woodstock, VT: Jewish Lights Publishing, 2008). Jews, he writes, should not attempt to defend themselves against the charge of being Christ-killers, since, in the New Testament, theology overrides history. He claims that Paul did not mean to foster anti-Semitism. This is probably correct, except that the apostle's anti-Jewish calumnies certainly added fuel to the fire. Rabbi Cook also defends Jesus by asserting (p. 44) that his violent invectives against the Pharisees were never uttered by him at all; they "reflect not the sentiments of Jesus – most likely a Pharisee himself – but solely those of the post-70 Gospel writers." Yet Jesus had ample reason to oppose the Pharisees, since they showed his messianic claims to be totally specious. Besides, if the words and deeds attributed to Jesus in the Gospel are not his, why take the New Testament seriously in the first place? Rabbi Cook does not seem to be especially interested in Jesus. His primary aim is to help his fellow Jews adapt to a Christian environment by softening the essential anti-Jewish thrust of the New Testament. Even the use of the word "Jews" in John's gospel is, according to the rabbi, purely symbolic (p. 225).

Minimizing Christian anti-Judaism is also the aim of *The Jewish Annotated New Testament* (New York: Oxford University Press, 2011), except that it is directed more to the Christian clergy than to Jews. Appended to this particular version (hereinafter JANT), edited by a team of Jewish scholars headed by Professors Amy-Jill Levine and Marc Zvi Brettler, is a series of essays purporting to explain the Judaism of the New Testament period. It seems odd that there is no entry on the Pharisees, who are not even mentioned in Prof. Levine's introduction entitled, "Bearing False Witness: Common Errors Made about Early Judaism." Perhaps the editors are so concerned about offending Christians that they prefer not to discuss the Pharisees, inasmuch as Jesus denounced them in no uncertain terms. Pious Christians would probably not like to learn that the Pharisees were virtuous people, since this could put Jesus in a bad light. Yet there is no getting around the fact that they are the authors of what is now considered normative Judaism. To appreciate Judaism at its true worth, one must first understand the Pharisees and the Pharisaic method.

The editors of JANT seem intent on presenting Jesus and The New Testament as a whole in the most favourable light possible. His insistence that he did not come to bring peace, but a sword (p. 21) seems to merit no comment whatsoever. Calling the Jews sons of the devil (p. 176) elicits only a brief note: "This verse is the source of the association of the Jews with Satan." Yes, but what does it tell us about Jesus? On this point, the silence of the editors is deafening. Concerning the "synagogue of Satan" (p. 469), they offer a convoluted theory that it does not refer to the Jews at all. They also assert (p. 52) that the tragically celebrated blood curse in Matthew 27, 25 was interpreted by the evangelist's early readers as applying only to the Jews of Jerusalem. No evidence is cited to support this claim. As for Paul's instructions to submit to the powers that be (p. 280), the editors hold that he was not referring to political authority, but to that of Jewish communal leaders. Yet in the first epistle of Peter (p. 439) we read that Christians must "accept the authority . . . of the emperor as supreme. . . ." This declaration elicits no comment in JANT.

In *The Misunderstood Jew: The Church and the Scandal of the Jewish Jesus* (New York: HarperCollins, 2007), Amy-Jill Levine undertakes to defuse Christian anti-Judaism by identifying Jesus squarely as a Jew. To judge by the reviews in some Christian journals, she has succeeded brilliantly. Even more impressive is her spirited defence of Judaism. As a feminist, she is especially perturbed about accusations that the Judaism of Jesus's time was oppressive to women. "To claim that Jesus 'liberated' women from a repressive Judaism by forbidding divorce is facile, wrong and bigoted." (p. 145) Prof. Levine adds that Paul forbade women to speak in church, to teach or to have authority over a man (pp. 90-91). She reminds us (pp. 128-129) that the God of the Jewish Bible often expresses love while that of the New Testament can be terribly wrathful.

No explanation of the Pharisees or their method can be found in *The Misunderstood Jew*, which is a pity since they are surely the most misunderstood Jews of all. The author concentrates instead on Jesus's vitriolic denunciations of them, which she finds "very Jewish" (p. 41). On this point, she is entirely correct – alas! It is common practice among Jews, especially Orthodox rabbis, to inveigh against coreligionists whose sense of piety is different from theirs. Rabbi Sacks once accused a Liberal confrere of destroying the faith. Among the Hasidim, rabbis regularly condemn those of other Hasidic sects as hypocrites, often with the adjective "godless" appended. Milton Himmelfarb compares Jesus to a Hasidic faith healer in a penetrating article entitled "On Reading Matthew," in *The Jews of Modernity* (New York: Basic Books, 1973) and concludes (p. 212) that "there are many similarities between early Christianity and Hasidism." He also argues, on the basis of Gospel texts (p. 206), that if the Pharisees were hypocrites, Jesus was no less so.

Concerning Jesus himself, the most complete survey is that of Joseph Klausner, *Jesus of Nazareth: His Life, Times and Teaching*, trans. Herbert Danby (New York: Macmillan, 1927). Klausner places his subject squarely in the Judaism of the time. An ardent Zionist, he admires Jesus for his nationalism, but adds that "Jesus was neither willing nor competent to declare war against Rome" (p. 313). While insisting on the essential Jewish character of Jesus, he adds pointedly that the Nazarene's teaching contains "a kernel of opposition to Judaism" (p. 369). From this kernel would sprout Christianity. Klausner is especially perceptive when he shows that Jesus's popularity in Galilee was in decline before he left for Jerusalem, where it finally collapsed.

Klausner cites approvingly a much earlier work written by Joseph Salvador, *Jésus-Christ et sa doctrine. Histoire de la naissance de l'église* (Paris: A. Guyot et Scribe, 1838). This truly pioneering study presents the Pharisees in their true light and explains how Jesus's insistence on the kingdom of heaven put him at odds with their teaching. The author views Christianity as a compromise between the moral code of Judaism and the other-worldliness of eastern religions. Salvador was not a Jew. He was born in the south of France to a non-observant Jewish father and a Catholic mother. At his request, he was buried in a Protestant cemetery. Yet throughout his adult life, he never ceased to defend Judaism against its numerous detractors. Those who believe that mixed marriages necessarily lead to Jewish assimilation may well take note.

In a remarkable work of erudition entitled *The Jewish Sources of the Sermon on the Mount* (London: Routledge, 1911) Gerald Friedlander, an English rabbi, explains that the Lord's Prayer and most of the Beatitudes are derived from the Bible or the Apocrypha. At the same time, he shows where and how Jesus deviated from Jewish teaching. The Nazarene disqualified himself as a prophet with his all-too-familiar "You have heard that it was said . . . but I say" since no prophet may introduce a new law in Judaism (p. 7). Rabbi Friedlander ably defends the Pharisees and declares their doctrine to be "infinitely superior to that of the Gospel" (p. 214). He extols their sense of tolerance in allowing Jesus to preach (p. 11) and reminds us that "the modern Jew . . . is also a Pharisee" (p. 101). In Chapter VI, entitled "Falsifying the Torah to Praise the Gospels", the defence of the Pharisees extends to the whole of Judaism, which he defines as "a simple system of ethics and not an intricate compendium of philosophy or theology" (p. 233). Rabbi Friedlander's book is now available as a reprint (ISBN 9781162757179) and is well worth reading.

David Flusser's *The Sage of Galilee: Rediscovering Jesus' Genius* (Grand Rapids, MI: Eerdmans, 2007) is a different piece of goods altogether. Flusser, an Israeli who taught early Christianity at the Hebrew University of Jerusalem, is positively infatuated with Jesus, whom he regards as a great moralist and prophet. He seems convinced that loving one's enemies is the very acme of ethical teaching (p. 74), equates the scribes and Pharisees with bigots (p. 39) and sides with Jesus on the crucial question of paying taxes to Rome (p. 46). Jesus, he claims, was the ally of social outcasts, especially the dreaded tax farmers (p. 82). Perhaps, but as social outcasts go, the tax farmers did very well for themselves. One of the author's redeeming qualities is that he has no use whatsoever for Pontius Pilate (pp.145-147). Here, Flusser's innate Judaism manages to shine through. For the rest, this is essentially a Christian interpretation of the Gospel.

In *Jesus the Jew: A Historian's Reading of the Gospels* (Philadelphia: Fortress Press, 1986), Geza Vermes similarly praises Jesus for defending "the pariahs of his world", such as tax farmers (p. 224). This comes as an afterthought, however, since the author is primarily concerned with showing that the Nazarene's ministry belonged to a charismatic Jewish tradition that was gradually "squeezed out" of normative Judaism by the rabbinate (p. 82). Vermes, professor of Jewish studies at Oxford, was not a historian; he earned his doctorate at the University of Louvain in theology. He correctly describes Jesus as an "exorcist, healer and itinerant preacher" (p. 29). In a companion volume entitled *Jesus in His Jewish*

Context (Minneapolis: Fortress Press, 2003), he claims some credit for the recent "change in the attitude of the churches to Judaism and the Jews." (p. 135).

For Hyam Maccoby, author of *Revolution in Judaea: Jesus and the Jewish Resistance* (London: Ocean Books, 1973), Jesus was something more: a rabbi and a prophet (pp. 135-150). This view is strongly contested by Levine (*The Misunderstood Jew*, p.132), who explains that a rabbi should be "focused on understanding the words of Torah and determining how to implement them." Maccoby cannot understand why Jesus, as a "rabbi," would have hurled insults at the Pharisees; so he posits that the offending passages in the Gospel were "doctored" later on by the evangelists (p. 139). The author sees Jesus as "a good man" who "fought not against some metaphysical evil but against Rome" (p. 255). He does admit, however, that the Nazarene had no armed force at his disposal (p. 189). His book is especially useful for its explanation of Judean opposition to Roman rule, as he reminds us that "the Jews alone, of all the nations conquered by Rome" resisted conquest for some 200 years (p. 69). An excellent introduction to Pharisaic reforms can be found as an appendix (pp. 275-282).

The tendancy among rabbis and other Jewish scholars to welcome Jesus into the fold is not new. Acording to a French Jesuit, Joseph Bonsirven, the current trend actually began in the late nineteenth century. His well-documented study, *Les juifs et Jésus. Attutude nouvelles* (Paris: Beauchesne, 1937), includes not only favourable references to the Nazarene, but also criticism. In particular, some Jewish observers cannot fail to note the differences between Jesus and the prophets of the Hebrew Bible, whose use of the first person singular always denotes God, speaking through them. By contrast, whenever Jesus says "I," he refers only to himself (p. 162). Bonsirven vigorously denounces the accusation of deicide leveled against the Jews by *"les gens du commun"* – the common people (p. 169). He regrets that those Jews who sympathize with Jesus seek to draw him closer to them, rather than drawing themselves closer to him (p. 213).

For Trude Weiss-Rosmarin, in *Judaism and Christianity, the Differences* (New York: The Jewish Book Club, 1943), the efforts on the part of some rabbis to reconcile the two value systems have gone too far. The Christian opposition to Judaism in such essential respects as sin and atonement, miracles, asceticism and faith in God makes such reconciliation impossible. She has no use for Jesus, whom she sees as being fundamentally hostile to Judaism and its approach to life. He is therefore neither a prophet nor a rabbi (pp. 126-151). Her book is a welcome retardant to the headlong rush on the part of many Jews to accept the New Testament and its central figure. It is now available as a reprint (ISBN 978-0-259-3279-6) and should be read by anyone who seeks to understand the Jewish-Christian contention.

More on the essential opposition between Judaism and Christianity can be found in Susannah Heschel's magisterial study, *Abraham Geiger and the Jewish Jesus* (Chicago: University of Chicago Press, 1998). Geiger, the leading liberal rabbi of his day, explained that since Jesus accomplished nothing, Christianity has to denigrate Judaism in order to elevate him (p. 196). He was not afraid to confront Protestant theologians, even when they accused him of offending Christians generally. Professor Heschel likewise pulls no punches. In a newspaper interview, she accuses Christianity of usurping the Jewish Scriptures and then denying the validity of Judaism. "It's a type of theological colonialism." *Ha'aretz*, 12 March 2009.

The Pharisees, and Jesus's vicious diatribes against them, remain the principal difficulty in portraying him as a devout Jew. Harvey Falk, an Orthodox rabbi, seeks a way out of this dilemma in *Jesus the Pharisee: A New Look at the Jewishness of Jesus* (Eugene, OR: Wipf and Stock, n.d.). In his view, Jesus was a Pharisee in the school of Hillel; his adversaries were followers of Shammai. Yet on the crucial issues of divorce and conversion to Judaism, both of which Jesus opposed, he was far closer to Shammai than to Hillel. Rabbi Falk sees in the anti-Pharisaic passages of the Gospels the roots of Christian anti-Semitism. He wonders whether Jesus was quoted correctly by the evangelists (p. 112). Perhaps not, but it is most unlikely that anti-Semites equate modern Jews with the Pharisees, since most Gentiles (and some Jews) believe that the Pharisees were an ancient Jewish sect that disappeared long ago.

In the interest of improved relations with Christians, many rabbis have embraced Jesus as one of their own. Among the most notable is Michael Lerner, an influential leader of Reform Judaism, who sees Jesus as "our brother, partner in Jewish renewal and part of the tradition of prophets, mystics, social activists and teachers who have for the past 2800 years been seeking to return Judaism to its highest vision and deepest truths." He implies that if Christians recognize Jesus as such, they will lose some of their hostility toward Judaism ("Jesus the Jew," *Tikkun*, May-June 2004, pp. 33-36). On a similar note, Levine hopes that Jesus can become a "bridge" between Jews and Christians (*The Misunderstood Jew*, p. 51). At present, the bridge seems to be open for one-way traffic only. The current infatuation with Jesus on the part of rabbis and Jewish academics may in time help reduce anti-Judaism among Christian theologians. It will not affect the growing number of atheists whose views on Jesus and Judaism are derived from Christianity. Worse, these well-meaning Jews could find themselves encouraging, albeit unwittingly, Jewish alienation, if not total apostasy.

The culmination of this trend – at least for now – is the book by Rabbi Shmuley Boteach, *Kosher Jesus* (Jerusalem: Gefen, 2012). It has been condemned without any possibility of appeal by his confreres of strict observance. Rabbi Yitzchok Wolf of Chicago refused to read the book; for him, the title was heretical enough. Rabbi Jacob Immanuel Schochet of Toronto summoned the author to withdraw his work from circulation and forbade any Jew to read it. Yet some did, including the present author, without being contaminated. As for Christians, whom Rabbi Boteach wants to enlist in a common effort to defend the State of Israel, their reaction has been decidedly tepid. Darrell Bock, professor of New Testament studies at the Dallas Theological Seminary, says that his coreligionists will not accept the rabbi's claim that Jesus was fully human. (See Mitchell Landsberg's article in the *Los Angeles Times*, 5 February 2012.) In contrast to the above-mentioned Orthodox rabbis, Lawrence H. Schiffman, professor of Judaic studies at Yeshiva University, uses reasoned argument to explain that Jesus was not a great teacher of Jewish ethics and that he "is best left to his Christian adherents." (See *Jewish Journal of Southern California*, February 24, 2012).

One Christian adherent particularly devoted to Jesus is André LaCoque, professor emeritus of the Hebrew Bible at the Chicago Theological Seminary. His book, *Jesus, the Central Jew: His Times and His People* (Atlanta: SBL Press, 2015) is basically an apology for the faith healer from Nazareth, whose centrality to Judaism is never demonstrated. The author's partiality can be seen in his bibliography, which includes seven books by Jacob Neusner, more than those of any other scholar, but not *A Rabbi Talks With Jesus*, which is surely the most relevant. He tries to define what he calls the "historical Jesus" (was there ever any other?) by inserting him "into the particular history of his environment." Yet there is little about Second Temple Judaism in this book. Professor LaCoque adds to the confusion by setting the "historical" Jesus in opposition to the "true" Jesus, whoever that may be (p. 5). A major difficulty here is that the author claims to be a historian (pp. 3 and 53), although he has no formal academic training in the discipline and seems oblivious to its purpose. He alludes to the baptism of Jesus as "most probably historical" (p. 193), when he should say "factual."

Another Christian Bible scholar who would like to be a historian is Bart D. Ehrman, professor of religious studies at the University of North Carolina. Actually, his specialty, in which he excels, is textual criticism. His book, *Jesus Interrupted: Revealing the Hidden Contradictions in the Bible and Why We Don't Know About Them* (New York: HarperOne, 2009) is devoted primarily to the New Testament. Although Professor Ehrman has no professional training in history, he does show an intuitive grasp of certain historical questions, in particular the importance of resurrection for the first Christians, who were in fact nationalistic Jews. They expected the Messiah to prevail over the Romans, but the occupying power "crushed him like a gnat" (p. 233). Only by believing in Jesus's resurrection could his Jewish followers remain loyal to him. The author does his Christian readers a great service by explaining how and why the early church fathers accentuated the initial anti-Jewish thrust of the New Testament (pp. 238-245).

Paula Fredriksen, professor of Scripture at Boston University, places the Jesus story squarely in the context of a Judea seething with revolt against Rome. In *Jesus of Nazareth: King of the Jews* (New York: Vintge Books, 1999), she notes with Josephus (p. 169) that the Temple authorities were subservient to imperial rule. At the same time, she doubts that Jesus actually "cleansed" anything (pp. 207-214). Given that Jesus had no armed force at his disposal, he posed no military threat to Rome. So why did Pilate bother to have him crucified? Professor Fredriksen gives a clear and convincing answer: the crucifixion was intended to serve as an object lesson to those Jews who might be tempted to take up arms against the occupiers of Judea (pp. 254-259).

In *A Rabbi Talks With Jesus* (2nd ed.; Montreal: McGill-Queen's University Press, 2000), Jacob Neusner engages Jesus in an amicable but frank conversation much as a Pharisee in ancient times might do, giving him the benefit of the doubt until he proclaims himself to be lord of the Sabbath. The author summarizes his findings in the preface, as he asserts (p. 5): "By the truth of the Torah, much that Jesus said is wrong." Neusner's honesty earned him the esteem of Cardinal Joseph Ratzinger, later Pope Benedict XVI, who devotes some twenty pages of his theological tome, *Jesus of Nazareth: From the Baptism in the Jordan to the Transfiguration* (New York: Doubleday, 2007) to the rabbi's book, whose arguments he attempts to refute. Both refuse to see the faith healer from Nazareth as just another Jewish social reformer. For the Pope, he is simply "the word of God in person" (p. 110). Benedict agrees with Rabbi Neusner that it is better for Jews and Christians to recognize their differences openly, rather than trying to sweep them under the carpet.

The Pope would probably not recommend a book written by two Gentiles, Gérard Mordillat and Jérôme Prieur, *Jésus contre Jésus* (Paris: Seuil, 1999). As its title suggests, this work of *haute vulgarisation* reveals the numerous contradictions in Jesus's teaching and in Christianity itself. How is it, the authors ask, that someone who claimed to preach love could encourage hatred of one's parents and foster conflict within the family (pp.

260-262)? And why did Christianity, which considers itself to be the religion of love, preach hatred of the Jews for centuries (pp. 332-333)? Jewish readers will particularly appreciate the comparison (p. 69) between the Hebrew Scriptures, in which several women express their wish to have children, and Jesus, who predicted that it would soon be said: "Blessed are the barren, and the wombs that never bore and the breasts that never nursed" (Lk. 23, 29). Judaism values life above all.

Inasmuch as Mordillat and Prieur are concerned with Jesus's opposition to himself, they take no account of his opposition to the Pharisees. In *From Politics to Piety: The Emergence of Pharisaic Judaism* (Englewood Cliffs, NJ: Prentice-Hall, 1973), Jacob Neusner seems to attribute most, if not all, of this hostility to the evangelists. With a touch of sarcasm, he finds the Pharisees "guilty of not having been Christians" (p. 68). The author notes that they were politically astute, as indeed they had to be in order to survive the devastation of Judea after the two failed insurrections against Rome. Their political awareness is surely evident in the question of paying taxes to Rome. Yet it is mentioned without comment (p. 69). Neusner asserts that little can be learned about the Pharisees by reading the Gospel, except that they were a table-fellowship sect (p. 80).

Actually, much can be learned about the Pharisees, *a contrario*, in the Gospel, as Claude Gruber-Magitot demonstrates in her magisterial essay, *Jésus et les pharisiens* (Paris: Laffont, 1964). She emphasizes their remarkable urbanity in dealing with the Nazarene's insults, as well their initial hospitality toward him (pp. 29-30). The questions they put to him are always courteous in tone (p. 417). The Pharisees' position concerning miracle cures performed on the Sabbath is explained patiently and convincingly (pp. 148-151). The author maintains that the morality of the Pharisees, which was impressed on all of Judaism, is a far better guide for living than that of Jesus. Thanks to Pharisaic interpretation, she writes, the Torah was able to evolve with the times, remaining "dynamic and vigorous, eternally young" (p. 133). Her infectious love for Judaism is most impressive.

Much of Ms. Gruber-Magitot's study is inspired by *The Pharisees* (new edition, Boston: Beacon Press, 1962) by the English scholar and Unitarian minister R. Travers Herford. He recognizes that the Pharisees developed rabbinical jurisprudence (*halacha*) "and kept it from becoming a rigid system" (p. 111). Christianity, he notes, has replaced *halacha* with dogma – hardly an improvement (p. 105). As for the prophetic books of the Bible, which are held in great esteem by Christians, the author explains that the Pharisees "never dreamed of repudiating prophetic teaching." On the contrary, "Pharisaism is applied prophesy." (p. 137) Herford recognizes that "rabbinical Judaism and Christianity are fundamentally irreconcilable" (p. 236) because of their opposing world-views. In his conclusion, he predicts that when Christianity has done all it can do, "there will then be a Judaism able and ready to offer its imperishable treasure, kept safe through the ages, to a world which will no longer scorn" (p. 238). Amen.

An excellent introduction to the differences between Judaism and Christianity can be found in "The Future of Jewish-Christian Relations", chapter 10 of *Futurizing the Jews: Alternative Futures for Meaningful Jewish Existence in the 21st Century* by Tsvi Bisk and Moshe Dror (Westport, CT: Praeger, 2003). Here, Jews are warned against "uncritical ecumenism" and accepting "the New Age bromide that all 'religions' are really the same" (p. 135). The authors concentrate not on theology, but on ethics, noting that Judaism emphasizes life on earth, for which Talmudic logic is a precious guide. In Judaism, redemption depends on moral worth, not divine grace (p. 152). To face the challenge of modern-day Christianity, Jews must replace "colourful ethnicity" (or what the authors call *Fiddler on the Roof* Judaism) with "uncompromising lucidity." (p. 154) This presupposes education.

In a series of articles published as *The Myth of the Judeo-Christian Tradition* (New York: Schocken, 1971), Arthur A. Cohen takes a largely philosophical and theological approach. The main bone of contention between Judaism and Christianity, he notes correctly, is the postulate: "If the Law saves [i.e. if the Torah is still valid], Christ dies for nothing" (p. 141). Despite the author's intellectual brilliance, his book shows its age. He asserts that because Judaism has not had power in the West, "it has never had the occasion of confusing power with justice or . . . mercy with the charity of kings" (p. 30). Oh, but it has – in the present-day State of Israel. His prime concern is the Church of Rome, which was undergoing great changes in the 1960s, when most of the articles were written. In our own time, the main challenge to Judaism comes not from Catholicism, but from the assimilationist tendencies of secular Christianity and the fervent missionary activity of evangelical Protestants.

On the question of intermarriage, sociologist Egon Mayer paints an optimistic picture in *Love and Tradition: Marriage Between Jews and Christians* (New York: Schocken, 1987). He notes with satisfaction that in the 1970s "unprecedented numbers of non-Jews were becoming Jewish by choice" (p 55) and that when the Gentile spouse converts to Judaism, the children are usually raised as Jews (pp. 253-260). His statistics are subject to revision, since current trends seem to indicate a disaffection from the synagogue, on the part not only of intermarrieds, but of endogamous couples as well. Membership dues and extra assessments just before the High Holy Days may be a factor, but there are surely others. Mayer records the frustration of a convert, who became "too Jewish" for her in-laws (pp. 241-242).

A similar problem is addressed in *Shiska: The Gentile Woman in the Jewish World* by Christine Benvenuto (New York: St. Martin's Press, 2004). Through a wide range of interviews, the author establishes beyond doubt that the main hindrance to the Gentile bride's adoption of Judaism is the confrontational attitude of her husband's family. Should she wish to convert, the Jewish parents will often question her sincerity; or else they may regard her as "a troublemaker who will make her man 'too Jewish' for his own family to recognize" (pp. 79-80).

Indeed, Jewish men have been known to complain that their formerly Christian wives are pushing them further into Judaism than they care to go (p. 174).

Ellen Jaffe McClain, in *Embracing the Stranger: Intermarriage and the Future of the American Jewish Community* (New York: Basic Books, 1995), places the entire question of intermarriage in the context of a Jewish identity based on vicarious suffering and a Jewish education that terminates at age 13 (pp. 111-114). But she remains sanguine, reminding us that Judaism was intensely missionary in ancient times and continues to attract interested Gentiles. She should know. Her husband of seven years decided, on his own, to convert to Judaism and was warmly received by members of the local synagogue (pp. 217-222). There is a moral here for those who wish to find one.

Notes

[1] R. Travers Herford, *Pharisaism: Its Aim and Method* (London: Williams & Norgate, 1912), p. 114.

[2] Richard Dawkins, *The God Delusion* (London: Black Swan, 2007), p. 283.

[3] Mt. 21.9.

[4] Salo Wittmayer Baron, *A Social and Religious History of the Jews*, vol. II: *Christian Era: The First Five Centuries* (New York: Columbia University Press, 1952), p. 70.

[5] A typical example is H. H. Ben-Sasson, ed., *A History of the Jewish People* (Cambridge, MA: Harvard University Press, 1976), which deals extensively with Judea under Roman rule but does not mention the ministry of Jesus or his compatriots' reaction to it.

[6] I.M. Choucroun, *Le judaïsme a raison* (2nd edition, Paris: Fondation Sefer, 1956).

[7] See, *inter alia*, Gerald Sigal, *The Jew and the Christian Missionary: A Jewish Response to Missionary Christianity* (New York: Ktav, 1981); Samuel Levine, *You Take Jesus, I'll Take God: How to Refute Christian Missionaries* (Los Angeles: Hamorah Press, 1980); Aryeh Kaplan *et al*, *The Real Messiah? A Jewish Response to Missionaries* (Toronto: Jews for Judaism, 2004); Chaim Picker, *"Make Us a God!" A Jewish Response to Hebrew Christianity* (New York: iUniverse, 2005).

[8] A leading historian of the period finds it plausible that "the general outline of his [Jesus'] career as presented in the Gospel biographies is correct." See Martin Goodman, *The Ruling Class of Judaea* (Cambridge: Cambridge University Press, 1987), pp. 22-23.

[9] Mt. 5.43-44.

[10] Ex. 23.4.

[11] Prov. 25.21.

[12] *Jerusalem Post*, 25 December 2001.

[13] Jonathan Freedland, "The story of Jesus is the ultimate political drama," *The Guardian*, 24 December 2011.

[14] Michael J. Cook, *Modern Jews Engage the New Testament: Enhancing Jewish Well-being in a Christian Environment* (Woodstock, VT: Jewish Lights Publishing, 2008), p. 57.

---

[15] See Susannah Heschel, *Abraham Geiger and the Jewish Jesus* (Chicago: University of Chicago Press, 1998), pp. 127 ff.

[16] Baron, *A Social and Religious History of the Jews*, Vol. II, *op. cit.*, p. 67.

[17] Irving Greenberg, *For the Sake of Heaven and Earth: The New Encounter between Judaism and Christianity* (Philadelphia: Jewish Publication Society, 2004), p. 153.

[18] Joseph Klausner, *Jesus of Nazareth: His Life, Times and Teaching*, trans. Herbert Danby (New York: Macmillan, 1927), p. 363.

[19] Ex. 21. 22-23.

[20] Mt. 5. 38-39.

[21] Jonathan Sacks, *The Politics of Hope* (London: Vintage, 2000), pp. 13, 26, 37, 93, 107, 219, 260-262, 268 *et passim*.

[22] *Jerusalem Post*, December 26, 2000.

[23] Jonathan Sacks, *Will We Have Jewish Grandchildren? Jewish Continuity and How To Achieve It* (London: Vallentine Mitchell, 1994), pp. 2 *et passim*.

[24] Sylvia Barack Fishman, *Double or Nothing? Jewish Families and Mixed Marriage* (Hanover, NH: Brandeis University Press, 2004), pp. 32-33.

[25] Jules Isaac, *Jesus and Israel*, trans, Sally Gran (New York: Holt, Rinehart and Winston, 1971).

[26] Mt. 10. 34-35.

[27] Mt. 8. 22.

[28] Mk. 11.12-14; Matt. 21.19.

[29] D. G. Littman, "Arafat and Jesus," *International Herald Tribune*, 4 April 1984.

[30] *La Republica* (Montevideo), 12 April 2011.

[31] Cf. *infra*, p. 25.

[32] *New York Times*, 10 April 2010.

[33] Mk. 16. 9.

[34] Judges 4. 4-12.

[35] Ruth, 1. 16.

[36] Esther 3. 20; 7. 1-6.

[37] Elisabeth Badinter, *L'amour en plus* (Paris: Flammarion, 1980), p. 18.

[38] Mt. 5.31; Mk. 10. 9.

[39] Deut. 24. 1-4.

[40] John Stuart Mill, *Nature and Utility of Religion* (New York: Liberal

Arts Press, 1958), p. 64, note 9.

[41] Lev. 19. 33-34.

[42] Ex. 23. 9; see also Deut. 10. 19.

[43] Mt. 10. 5-7.

[44] Mt. 6. 7.

[45] Mt. 23. 15.

[46] Mt. 7. 6.

[47] Mk. 7. 25-29.

[48] Lk. 14. 26.

[49] Deut. 30. 19.

[50] Philip Goodman, *The Rosh Hashanah Anthology* (Philadelphia: Jewish Publication Society, 1992), p. 62.

[51] Mt. 7. 1.

[52] *Pirkei Aboth*, 2. 5.

[53] Mt. 5. 38-39.

[54] Dawkins, *The God Delusion,* p. 283.

[55] Nayyar Pyarelal, *Mahatma Gandhi: The Last Phase* (2 vols.; Ahmedabad: Navajivan Publishing House, 1956-58), Vol. II, p. 326.

[56] Mt. 10, 33.

[57] Lam. 3. 30.

[58] Ex. 21. 24.

[59] Fred R. Shapiro, ed., *The Yale Book of Quotations* (New Haven: Yale University Press, 2006), pp. 269-270.

[60] *The Independent* (London), 15 August 2000.

[61] Lev. 19.18.

[62] Prov. 20.22.

[63] Raphaël Draï, *Le mythe de la Loi du Talion. Une introduction au droit hébraïque* (Aix-en-Provence: Alinéa, 1991), pp. 222-229 *et passim*.

[64] Lev. 24. 19-20.

[65] Michel Renaud, « Connaissances du judaïsme: la loi du talion », *Un echo d'Israël* (November-December 2005) ; Rabbi Ben Lankton, "An Eye For $100, A Tooth For About Ten Bucks: The Monetary Meaning of Mishpatim", http://www.lyjewishlearning.com/texts:Weekly_Torahcommentary/ mishpatim_hill...

[66] Max Domarus, ed. Hitler. *Reden und Proklamationen* (3 vols.; Munich: SüddeutscherVerlag, 1973), II, 1058.

[67] *Ibid.*, III, 828-829; cf.Eliahu Ben Elissar, *La diplomatie du IIIe Reich et*

---

les juifs (Paris: Julliard, 1968), p. 473.

[68] Mt. 5. 43-44.

[69] Deut. 30. 19.

[70] *Aboth* of Rabbi Nathan, ch. 23.

[71] Deut. 23. 8.

[72] Jn. 2. 4.

[73] Jn. 8.31 and 44.

[74] Joshua Trachtenberg, *The Devil and the Jews: The Medieval Conception of the Jew and its Relation to Modern Antisemitism* (New York: Meridian Books, 1961).

[75] Mt. 23. 13-15, 23, 25, 27-28; also Lk. 11 44

[76] Mt. 23.16.

[77] Mt. 23.33-35, 12.34.

[78] Lk. 11. 40.

[79] Mt. 23. 17.

[80] Mt. 5. 22.

[81] Mt. 5, 17.

[82] The sacrificial cult is described in Ezekiel, 43:18-27.

[83] Kaufmann Kohler, "Pharisees," *Jewish Encyclopedia* (New York: Ktav, 1975), pp. 661-666.

[84] Ex. 20, 8-10.

[85] Stuart E. Rosenberg, *The Christian Problem: A Jewish View* (New York: Hippocrene Books, 1986), p. 134.

[86] Deut. 5, 14.

[87] Charles Guignebert, *Le monde juif vers le temps de Jésus* (Paris: Albin Michel, 1935), pp. 100-101.

[88] R. Travers Herford, *The Pharisees* (Boston: Beacon Press, 1962), p. 54.

[89] See, *inter allia*, Daniel-Rops, *La vie quotidienne en Palestine au temps de Jésus* (Paris : Hachette, 1961), p. 505 ; Roland H. Bainton, *Christianity* (New York: Mariner Books, 2000), p. 38.

[90] Gen. 4, 9.

[91] *Talmud Bavli*, Baba Mezi'a 62a.

[92] Jacob Neusner, *From Politics to Piety: The Emergence of Pharisaic Judaism* (Englewood Cliffs, NJ: Prentice-Hall, 1973), p. 83.

[93] Mk. 7, 4.

[94] Lk. 11, 37-40; see also Lk. 7, 36.

[95] See in particular Matt. 23, 13-15, 23, 25, 27, 28,

[96] For example, Maureen Dowd, "Pharisees on the Potomac," *New York Times*, 18 July 2009. The headline may not have been written by Ms. Dowd, but by editors of the *Times* op-ed page. See Philologos, "The New York Times: Ignorant and Antisemitic?" *Forward*, 7 August 2009.

[97] *Pirkei Aboth*, 2. 18.

[98] Mk. 7, 5-8.

[99] Mk. 7, 19.

[100] Mt. 12, 8.

[101] Gen. 2, 2-3.

[102] Jacob Neusner, *A Rabbi Talks With Jesus* (2nd ed., Montreal: McGill-Queen's University Press, 2000), p. 87.

[103] Joseph Salvador, *Jésus-Christ et sa doctrine. Histoire de la naissance de l'église* (Paris : A. Guyot et Scribe, 1838), pp. 364-368.

[104] Lk. 18, 29-30.

[105] Jn. 3, 1.

[106] This fact is duly noted by Herford, *The Pharisees*, pp. 205-206.

[107] Jn. 8, 3-11.

[108] Bart D. Ehrman, *Misquoting Jesus: The Story Behind Who Changed the Bible and Why* (New York: HarperCollins, 2005), pp. 63-65.

[109] Lev. 20, 10; Deut. 22, 22.

[110] Kohler, "Pharisees", *loc. cit.*, p. 662; André LaCoque and Paul Ricoeur, *Thinking Biblically: Exegetical and Hermeneutical Studies* (Chicago: University of Chicago Press, 1998), p. 97 .

[111] Mt. 7, 1.

[112] Mk 10, 9; I Cor. 7, 10-11; Matt. 5, 32.

[113] Deut. 24, 1-2.

[114] Mt. 5, 18.

[115] *VaYikra Rabba*, 8: 1.

[116] Mt. 10, 1.

[117] Mk. 2, 7; Lk. 5, 21.

[118] C. S. Lewis, *Mere Chrisianity* (New York: HarperCollins, 1972), pp. 51-52

[119] Mt. 23, 25-33.

[120] Mk. 12, 29-32.

[121] Lk. 20, 47.

[122] Ex. 22, 21.

[123] Deut. 24, 17.

---

[124] Lk. 16, 14.

[125] Josephus, *Antiquities of the Jews*, Book XVIII, chapter 1, paragraph 3.

[126] Baron, *A Social and Religious History of the Jews,* vol. I, pp. 174-175.

[127] Ps. 15, 3.

[128] Mt. 27, 11

[129] Klausner, *Jesus of Nazareth, op. cit.,* p. *259.*

[130] Mt. 16, 13-16.

[131] Salvador, *Jésus-Christ et sa doctrine*, pp. 226-227.

[132] Is. 45, 1.

[133] Lk. 9, 18.

[134] *Pirkei Aboth*, 2. 6.

[135] Mt. 4, 23.

[136] Joel Carmichael, "The Jesus Story and the Jewish War," *Midstream* (April 1979), p. 66.

[137] Mt. 1.1-17.

[138] Lk. 1, 27.

[139] Lk. 4. 23-38.

[140] Yankel Mandel, *Dictionnaire des Messies juifs* (Paris: Berg International, 2009).

[141] Mt. 1, 22.

[142] Is. 7, 14.

[143] Milton Himmelfarb, "On Reading Matthew," *The Jews of Modernity* (New York: Basic Books, 1973), p. 200.

[144] II Cor. 3, 15.

[145] Claude Gruber-Magitot, *Jésus et les pharisiens* (Paris: Laffont, 1964), p. 411.

[146] Mt. 23, 9.

[147] Mt. 12, 46-50.

[148] Marc Bloch, *Les rois thaumaturges* (Paris: Colin, 1961).

[149] *Talmud Bavli*, Baba Mezi'a 59b.

[150] Mt. 12. 10-13.

[151] Lk. 13, 11-12.

[152] Lk. 14, 2-4.

[153] Lk. 13, 14.

[154] Mt. 12, 11 ; Lk. 14, 5.

[155] Lk. 11, 20.

[156] Gerald Friedlander, *The Jewish Sources of the Sermon on the Mount* (London: Routledge, 1911), pp. 152-165 *et passim*.

[157] Mt. 6, 7.

[158] Mt. 6, 32-33.

[159] Mt. 5, 46-47.

[160] Lk. 3, 13.

[161] Is. 49, 15.

[162] Is. 53, 5.

[163] Is. 2, 3-4.

[164] Mt. 10, 5.

[165] Mt. 5, 20.

[166] Mk. 10, 21.

[167] Lk. 16, 19-26.

[168] Mk. 14, 7.

[169] Deut. 15, 11.

[170] Cf. *Infra*, p. 67.

[171] Mt. 19, 24-25.

[172] *Pirkei Aboth* 4, 1

[173] Mt. 19, 10-12.

[174] Deut. 14, 1; 23, 1; Lev. 19, 28.

[175] Abba Hillel Silver, *Where Judaism Differed: An Inquiry into the Distinctiveness of Judaism* (New York: Macmillan, 1956), pp. 232-237.

[176] Mt. 4, 24-25.

[177] Mt. 14, 25.

[178] Jn. 2, 1-11.

[179] Lk. 5, 1-9.

[180] Mk. 5, 41-44.

[181] Mk. 4, 35-41.

[182] Lk. 13, 31-33.

[183] Lk. 18, 35-43; Mk. 10, 46-52.

[184] Mt. 21, 8-9.

[185] Mt. 13, 57 ; Mk. 6, 3.

[186] Jn. 8, 11.

[187] Jn. 14, 6.

[188] Micah 6, 8.

[189] Jn. 6, 66.

[190] Jn. 7, 5.

[191] Mt. 6, 28-32.

[192] Mk. 2, 15.

[193] Lk. 5, 29.

[194] Mt. 21, 31.

[195] Lk. 18, 9-14.

[196] Lk. 5, 30.

[197] George Foot Moore, *Judaism in the First Centuries of the Christian Era* (2 vols.; New York: Schocken, 1971), vol. I, pp. 58, 287-288.

[198] Mk. 11, 11.

[199] Lk. 19, 5-8.

[200] Mt. 10, 34.

[201] Mt. 10, 35-36.

[202] Mal. 3, 24.

[203] See Jn. 10, 19.

[204] Lk. 22, 66-67.

[205] Mk. 8, 11-12.

[206] Mt. 24, 7-8.

[207] Mt. 26, 69-74 ; Mk. 14, 66-68.

[208] Mk. 11, 13.

[209] Mt. 21, 19.

[210] Cf. Albert Réville, *Jésus de Nazareth* (Paris: Fischbacher, 1879), pp. 69-70; Paula Fredriksen, *Jesus of Nazareth, King of the Jews* (New York: Knopf, 2000), p. 115.

[211] Pierre Batiffol, *L'enseignement de Jésus* (Paris: Bloud, 1909), p. 877; cf. Karl Adam, *Jésus le Christ*, trans. E. Ricard (Paris: Casterman, 1934), p. 130.

[212] http://www.mountainretreatorg.net/sermons/whydidjesuscurseth efigtree.html

[213] See Baron, *A Social and Religious History of the Jews*, vol. I, *op. cit.*, pp.171-179.

[214] Marcel Simon, *Verus Israël. Etude sur les relations entre chrétiens et juifs dans l'empire romain, 135-425* (Paris: de Boccard, 1964), pp. 250-263.

[215] Bernard Gui, *Manuel de l'inquisiteur* (2 vols., Paris: Champion, 1926-1927), vol. II, pp. 6-9.

[216] Aimé Pallière, *Le sanctuaire inconnu. Ma « conversion » au judaïsme* (Paris: Rieder, 1926), p. 172. (italics in original).

[217] Yuri Slezkine, *The Jewish Century* (Princeton, NJ: Princeton University Press, 2004); Andrew R Heinze, *Jews and the American Soul*

(Princeton, NJ: Princeton University Press, 2004).

[218] See, *inter allia*, Jacques-Bénigne Bossuet, *Discours sur l'histoire universelle* (Paris: Fume, 1847), pp. 323 *et passim*.

[219] Jn. 7, 49.

[220] Mk. 12, 35; Lk. 19, 47.

[221] G. George Fox, *The Jews, Jesus and Christ* (Chicago: Argus Books, 1953), p. 46.

[222] Mt. 21, 23 ; Lk. 20, 2.

[223] Deut. 20, 219-20.

[224] Mt. 26, 4; Lk. 19, 47.

[225] Jn. 7, 1.

[226] Mk. 12, 28-32.

[227] Deut. 6, 4; Lev. 19, 18.

[228] Jn. 8, 31 and 44.

[229] Geza Vermes, *The Religion of Jesus the Jew* (Minneapolis: Fortress Press, 1993), p. 213.

[230] Jn. 8, 41.

[231] André LaCocque, *Jesus the Central Jew: His Times and His People* (Atlanta: SBL Press, 2015), p. 158.

[232] Jn. 2, 19-21.

[233] Lk. 2, 24.

[234] Mt. 21,13.

[235] Jn. 2, 14-15.

[236] Mt. 21, 12.

[237] Gordon W. Prange, ed., *Hitler's Words* (Washington: American Council on Public Affairs, 1944), p. 71.

[238] See Mk. 14, 12.

[239] Jn. 19, 7.

[240] Mc. 14, 61-62.

[241] Mt. 26, 14-16 ; Lk. 22, 3-6.

[242] Jn. 12, 6.

[243] Susan Gubar, *Judas: A Biography* (New York: Norton, 2009), pp. 6, 131-132, 276; for Karl Barth, see Jeremy Cohen, *Christ Killers: The Jews and the Passion from the Bible to the Big Screen* (New York: Oxford University Press, 2007), pp. 259-260.

[244] Hyam Maccoby, *Judas Iscariot and the Myth of Jewish Evil* (New York: Free Press, 1992), pp. 120-122.

[245] Gubar, *Judas, op. cit.*, pp. 263-264.

[246] Lk. 22, 52-53.
[247] Mt. 26, 56 and 74.
[248] Jn. 11, 48.
[249] Jn. 14, 6.
[250] Mk. 12, 17 ; Lk. 20, 25.
[251] Mt. 22, 18.
[252] Mt. 23, *passim*.
[253] Lk. 11, 23.
[254] Flavius Josephus, *The Jewish War*, vol. I, trans. Henry St. John Thackaray (Cambridge MA, Harvard University Press, 1997), p. 389
[255] Jean-Pierre Lémonon, *Pilate et le gouvernement de la Judée* (Paris: Lecoffre, 1981), pp. 163-168.
[256] Lk. 13, 1.
[257] Mt. 27, 26.
[258] Mk. 15, 26.
[259] Lk. 23, 27-28.
[260] Cf. *supra*, p. 9.
[261] Josephus, *The Jewish War, op. cit.*, pp. 351, 419 and 443.
[262] Lk. 23, 25.
[263] Jn. 18, 36.
[264] Mt. 27, 46.
[265] Jn. 19, 40.
[266] Mt. 16, 18.
[267] Gérard Mordillat and Jérôme Prieur, *Jésus après Jésus. L'origine du christianisme* (Paris: Seuil, 2004), pp. 37-39.
[268] Mt. 18, 15-17.
[269] Lk. 24, 5.
[270] Gérard Mordillat and Jérôme Prieur, *Jésus contre Jésus* (Paris: Seuil, 1999), pp. 154-162.
[271] Lk. 24, 21. The usual translation reads that he would "redeem" Israel. This must be understood in a Jewish sense, as in redeeming a captive.
[272] Acts 1, 6.
[273] Acts 2, 46-47.
[274] Acts 22, 28.
[275] Acts 6, 8 – 7, 60.
[276] Acts 9, 20-21.
[277] I Cor. 15, 16-17.

[278] Acts 13, 46.

[279] Rom. 13, 1.

[280] Ps. 146, 3.

[281] Zec. 4, 6.

[282] Mic. 4, 2.

[283] *Pirkei Aboth*, 1, 10.

[284] *Ibid.*, 2, 3.

[285] See Tacitus, *Annals*, Book XV.

[286] I Thess. 2, 15-16.

[287] Mordillat and Prieur, *Jésus après Jésus, op. cit.*, pp. 237-238

[288] John Wesley, *Explanatory Notes Upon the New Testament* (4th ed., New York: Lane & Scott, 1850), p. 527.

[289] http://www.thedenverchannel.com/news/2873395/detail.html

[290] Michel de Jaeghere, "Religieusement correct," *Le Figaro*, 10 March 2004.

[291] Mt. 27, 25-35.

[292] Tacitus, *The Annals*, book 15 chapter 44; cf. Joseph Bonsirven, *Les juifs et Jésus. Attitudes nouvelles* (Paris: Beauchesne, 1937), p. 169.

[293] Lk. 24, 20.

[294] Acts, 2, 23.

[295] Acts 4, 27.

[296] Acts 4, 10.

[297] Acts 5, 30.

[298] Acts 10, 39.

[299] I Cor. 7, 10.

[300] II Cor. 5, 16.

[301] I Cor. 1, 23.

[302] Gen. 22, 10-12.

[303] Gal. 3, 13.

[304] Acts. 19, 10

[305] Acts 13, 43.

[306] See, *inter allia*, Johann August Neander, *General History of the Christian Religion and the Church*, trans. Joseph Torrey (London: Wiley & Putnam, 1849), vol. I, p. 67.

[307] Ex. 20, 10.

[308] Josh. 8, 35.

[309] I Cor. 9, 20.

[310] Acts 13, 15.

---

[311] Acts 13, 17-29.

[312] Acts, 13, 44-45.

[313] Acts 14, 1.

[314] Acts 17, 1-8.

[315] Acts 19, 8.

[316] Rom. 7, 7-8.

[317] Elizabeth Fox-Genovese, "A Conversion Story," *First Things* (April 2000), pp. 39-43.

[318] Ex. 20, 1-17.

[319] Rom. 5, 18.

[320] Baron, *A Social and Religious History of the Jews, op. cit.*, vol. I, pp. 4-10; cf. infra, pp. 102, 139.

[321] I Cor. 7, 1.

[322] Gen. 1, 28.

[323] I Cor. 7, 8.

[324] *Talmud Bavli*, Zohar Hadash, IV, 50b.

[325] Acts 16, 1-3.

[326] Gal. 5, 2.

[327] Aaron A. R. Tobian and Ronald H. Gray, "The Medical Benefits of Male Circumcision," *Journal of the American Medical Association* (5 October 2011), pp. 1479-1480.

[328] Baron, *A Social and Religious History of the Jews, op. cit.*, vol. I, pp. 6-7.

[329] Rom. 6, 5.

[330] Gal. 3, 28

[331] Col. 3, 18-22.

[332] Rom. 2, 14.

[333] See, *inter allia*, Rom. 3, 24; II Cor. 8, 9; Gal. 1, 15; II Tim. 2, 1.

[334] *U. S. A. Today*, 22 April 2007.

[335] I Pet. 2, 9.

[336] Darell Bock, "The Politics of the People of God," *Christianity Today*, 7 September 2005.

[337] George C. Papademetriou, "The People of God: An Orthodox Perspective," http://www.goarch.org/ourfaith/ourfaith9285.

[338] Ex. 19, 5.

[339] Papademetriou, *loc. cit.*

[340] Deut. 7, 7.

[341] Is. 53, 3.

---

[342] Hab. 2, 4.

[343] Gal. 3, 11.

[344] Acts 5, 34-39.

[345] Acts 23, 9.

[346] Acts 27, 22.

[347] See Simon, *Verus Israel, op. cit.*

[348] In proposition 30. For the complete text, see
http://www.ewtn.com/library/encyc/p12mysti.htm

[349] Lawrence H. Schiffman, *Who Was a Jew: Rabbinic and Halakhic Perspectives on the Jewish-Christian Schism* (Hoboken, NJ: Ktav, 1985), pp. 51-53, 67.

[350] *Ibid.*, p. 75; cf. Baron, *A Social and Religious History of the Jews, op. cit.*, vol. II, p. 132.

[351] I Thess. 2, 16.

[352] I Pet. 2, 8-9.

[353] Rev. 3, 9.

[354] II Cor. 3, 7.

[355] See, for example, A. Roy Eckhardt, *Elder and Younger Brothers: The Encounter of Jews and Christians* (New York: Schocken, 1973); Mary C. Boys, *Has God Only One Blessing? Judaism as a Source of Christian Self-Understanding* (New York: Paulist Press, 2000).

[356] It may be viewed on the Vatican website.

[357] Donald Senior, "Rome Has Spoken: A New Catholic Approach to Judaism," *Commonweal*, 31 January 2003, pp. 20-23.

[358] Youness Bousenna, « Les pharisiens ou l'histoire d'un préjugé », *Le Monde*, 14 April 2021.

[359] Catherine Marciano, « Le pape François rappelé à l'ordre concernant ses propos sur les pharisiens », *Le Devoir*, 13 May 2019.

[360] Amy-Jill Levine, *The Misunderstood Jew: The Church and the Scandal of the Jewish Jesus* (San Francisco: HarperCollins, 2006), pp. 11-13.

[361] Jn. 14, 6.

[362] Ps. 19.15.

[363] Mt. 27, 25.

[364] Lk. 23, 34; for the 10 points, see
http://www.jcrelations.net/An+Adress+to+the+Churches.

[365] *Forward*, 12 February 2012.

[366] Francis Weill, *Juifs et chrétiens. Requiem pour un divorce* (Paris:

L'Harmattan, 2001), p. 424.

[367] The Pew Forum on Religion & Public Life, *U. S. Religious Landscape Survey, Report 1: Religious Affiliation,* http://religions.pewforum./org/reports.

[368] *Le Figaro,* 18 November 2011.

[369] *New York Times,* 16 January 1999.

[370] Karl Barth, *Church Dogmatics* (London: T. & T. Clark International, 1957), vol. II, part 2, p. 209.

[371] *Ibid.,* pp. 264 and 288.

[372] *Ibid.,* p. 298.

[373] Deut. 4, 6.

[374] Deut. 23, 7.

[375] Frank Riess, "From Aachen to Al-Andalus: the journey of Deacon Bodo", *Early Medieval Europe,* 2005 (2), pp. 131-157.

[376] Julie G. Fax "Rabbi Capers Funnye battles to open the gates of Judaism," *Jewish Journal of Southern California,* 26 November 2008; Zev Chafets, "Obama's Rabbi," *New York Times Magazine,* 9 April 2009.

[377] Is. 56, 7.

[378] Lk. 2, 4-15.

[379] Mt. 2 , 15.

[380] Hos. 11, 1

[381] Ex. 4, 22.

[382] Ps. 2, 7; Heb. 1, 5 ;

[383] Armand Abécassis, « *En vérité je vous les dis.* » *Une lecture juive des évangiles* (Paris Edition °1, 1999), p. 260.

[384] Is. 7, 14.

[385] Is. 53, *passim.*

[386] Daniel Boyarin, *The Jewish Gospels: The Story of the Jewish Christ* (New York: The New Press, 2012), pp. 152-155 .

[387] *Aboth of Rabbi Nathan,* B 31.

[388] Mic. 1, 5; 4, 1-2.

[389] Yaakov Ariel, *Evangelizing the Chosen People: Missions to the Jews in America, 1880-2000* (Chapel Hill, NC: University of North Carolina Press, 2000), pp. 197-199.

[390] http://www.olivetreefund.org/life-from-the-dead.php.

[391] Pope John Paul II, *Crossing the Threshold of Hope* (New York: Knopf, 1994), p. 183.

392http://www.betrue.org/resources/pdf/Jewish_Response_to_Missio
naries.pdf.

393 Sigal, *The Jew and the Christian Missionary, op. cit.*

394 See Emil. L. Fackenheim, *The Jewish Return Into History: Reflections
in the Age of Auschwitz and a New Jerusalem* (New York: Schocken,
1978), pp. 31-32.

395 Alan Dershowitz, *The Vanishing American Jew* (New York: Simon &
Schuster, 1979), pp. 294-295.

396 Jeffrey Kleinman, "A call for a return to Judaism's didactic roots,"
Princeton Alumni Weekly, July 2, 2003.

397 Ariel, *Evangelizing the Chosen People, op. cit.*, p. 272.

398http://www.jewsforjudaism.org/index.php?option=com.content&vi
ew=article&id=270:jerusalem-office-press-release&catid=59.

399 *Canadian Jewish News*, 23 October 2017.

400 Jeremy Rosen, *Understanding Judaism* (Edinburgh: Dunedin
Academic Press, 2003), p. 133.

401 Kravitz, *Jewish Response to Missionaries, op. cit.*, p. 52.

402 *Ibid.*, pp. 49-51.

403 The sermon was repeated in 2003. See "Parasha Commentary,"
JSTA Distance Learning Project, 10 July 10 2003.

404 Ex. 34, 15-16.

405 Ernest Gugenheim, *Les portes de la loi. Etudes et responsa* (Paris:
Albin Michel, 1962), p. 145.

406 Num, 12, 1.

407 Ex. 32, *passim.*

408 Levine, *The Misunderstood Jew, op. cit.*, pp. 160-161.

409 Boyarin, *The Jewish Gospels, op. cit.*, pp. 102 ff.

410 Shmuley Boteach, *Kosher Jesus* (Jerusalem: Gefen, 2012), p. 24.

411 Mt. 5, 38-43.

412 Lk. 14, 26.

413 Mk. 11, 13.

414 Mt. 21, 31.

415 Lk. 20, 25.

416 Mt. 12, 1-8.

417 Boteach, *Kosher Jesus, op. cit.*, p. 206.

418 Will Pavia in *The Times* (London), 7 February 2012.

419 Boteach, *Kosher Jesus, op. cit.*, p. 213; Sacks, *The Politics of Hope,
op. cit.*, pp. 13, 26, 37, 93, 95, 107, 219, 238, 260-262 *et passim.*

[420] Boteach, *Kosher Jesus*, p. 213.

[421] Jacob Neusner, *Jews and Christians: The Myth of a Common Tradition* (London: SCM Press, 1991), p. 120.

[422] Bart D. Ehrman *Jesus, Interrupted: Reading the Hidden Contradictions in the Bible and Why We Don't Know About Them* (New York: HarperOne, 2009), p. 257.

[423] Mt. 9, 20; Lk. 8, 44.

[424] Ex. 34, 33-35.

[425] *II Cor. 3, 12-16.*

[426] Boyarin, *The Jewish Gospels, op. cit.*, p. 21.

[427] See his *Epistle to Yemen*, written in 1172.

[428] Cf. *supra*, p. 18.

[429] Jer. 16, 11.

[430] See Simeon J. Maislin, *And Turn It Again: Theme and Sacred Variations* (Dartford: Xlibris, 2008), p. 216.

[431] Baron, *A Social and Religious History of the Jews, op. cit.*, vol. I, pp. 4-10.

[432] René Rémond, *Le christianisme en accusation* (Paris: Albin Michel, 2005), pp. 71-83, 114.

[433] Rom. 6, 3-4.

[434] Rabbi Jeremy Rosen, "Marrying Out," http://www.somethingjewish.co.uk/articles/1521marryingout.htm

[435] *Talmud yerushalmi*, Kiddushin 4, 1 65b.

[436] Kravitz, *The Jewish Response to Missionaries, op. cit.*, pp. 43-46.

[437] For two opposite examples, see Egon Mayer, *Love and Tradition: Marriage Between Jews and Christians* (New York, Schocken, 1987), pp. 198-201.

[438] Halford R. Ryan, *Franklin D. Roosevelt's Rhetorical Presidency* (New York: Grenwood Press, 1988), pp. 16, 79-80.

[439] Tsvi Bisk and Moshe Dror, *Futurizing the Jews: Alternative Futures for Meaningful Jewish Existence in the 21st Century* (Westport, CT: Praeger, 2003), pp. 150-151.

[440] Hos. 6, 6.

[441] Mt. 26, 26-28 ; Mk. 14, 22-24, Lk. 22, 19-20 ; I Cor. 11, 23-25.

[442] Charles Guignebert, *Jesus*, trans. S. H. Hooke (New York: Knopf, 1935), pp. 302, 435, 441, 447. The author doubts that Jesus sought to establish a new covenant.

[443] Jn. 6, 56-60.

---

[444] Lev. 17, 10-12.
[445] Jn. 8, 32.

Printed in Great Britain
by Amazon

41878534R00106